To: Star
From Randall R.
good reading
June 8 '2A 23

MW01267631

About
GROWING RICH: Success in Business, Success in Life

The Randall Baskin story is one that I would want every Belmont student to understand. Here's a man who gave the most extraordinary effort in building a tremendously successful business while at the same time giving the same high level of attention to the building of a successful family, spiritual, and civic life. Randall Baskin is living proof that God really does want us to have a good life.

—Bob Fisher, President, Belmont University

If I didn't know Randall, I would think his story was fiction. How could one man, without the resources we think are necessary for success, accomplish all that he did? This book is the story of how Randall discovered some of life's most important secrets and applied them to his life. I've heard most of these stories over lunch with him. You'll leave this book the same way I leave those lunches wondering to yourself, "If he did all of that with his life, what can I do with mine?"

—Mike Glenn, senior pastor, Brentwood Baptist Church, Brentwood, TN

Andrew Carnegie's magic formula brought fortunes to those to whom he disclosed his secret, and this was the inspiration for Napoleon Hill. Napoleon Hill's secret of true and lasting success revealed in *Think and Grow Rich* motivated millions since its publication in 1937, and was a central, guiding force for Randall Baskin. Randall Baskin brought this inspiration to thousands in his life, not only showing what to do but how to do it, and this book tells his story.

—James Nichols; Vice President, Morgan Stanley Smith Barney

Business schools don't teach that the most important law of success is that you have to give in order to receive. Randall Baskin does it and teaches it.

—Calvin Lehew, author, businessman

Randall Baskin's book *Growing Rich* is much more than a manual on how to get rich, although I'm sure it will be that for countless sales professionals and businesspersons. In his down-home storytelling style, as if he were sitting beside you as he whittles a bit of cedar, you'll hear a rags-to-riches story that inspires your soul to say, "Gosh... I could do that, too!" But as the pages and stages of his life unfold, you will also mature into a joyful giver—realizing where life's true riches are stored. In its chapters I found eternal spiritual principles which, if applied to one's business life or the everyday business of living, will result in treasures beyond measure.

—Peter Shockey, author, *Reflections of Heaven & Journey Of Light*

Randall Baskin's inspiring poverty-to-prosperity story *Growing Rich* will ignite the passion of anyone who is ready to turn their own challenges and adversities into greatness. Should be required reading for all salesmen!

—Stowe D Shockey, author, *Flying High*

Randall Baskin's *Growing Rich* is a testimony of inspiration and a "how-to" book for entrepreneurs, account managers, business and faith leaders and anyone who loves a story of hardship and success. From humble beginnings to an incredible life of financial success, Mr. Baskin's determination to succeed has given him the opportunity to share generously and bless thousands of people along the way. He shares the principles and true-life experiences that have been the driving force behind his business success and his motivation for helping people believe in themselves.

Mr. Baskin's lifelong compilation of Bible verses and inspirational sayings gleaned from the works of others is a priceless collection that will motivate you to discover your own potential toward a journey of achievement and charity. You'll appreciate an honest account of Randall's life, from the highest peaks of triumph to the lowest ebbs of sadness and loss. In this, he reveals how his faith in God has carried him through difficult days and taught him that life's greatest joy comes from giving. Having the privilege of knowing Randall Baskin for over 40 years, his story is as real as he described, a genuine account of a great American success story.

—Steve Durham, Senior Pastor, Sunset Hills Baptist Church

One of the greatest moments of my life was in November 1962 when I met Randall Baskin. Upon completing my service in the army, I was excited to get my career started. Fortunately, while looking for a job, I met Randall Baskin. I went to work for Randall, whose wisdom and knowledge helped change my life. Randall became my motivator, mentor, and friend over the years. After 50 years,

I can honestly say that I have seen a man who began with nothing, yet became a multimillionaire by using the great principles of selling and ethics. He read many motivational books, which he encouraged me to read as well. Watching him believe in himself, inspired me to do the same.

Over the past years I have encouraged Randall to write this book because his wisdom should be shared with everyone, from the high school freshman to the seasoned business person. This book is a must-read guideline to success for all ages. My deepest gratitude goes to Randall, who has shown that with faith and the desire to succeed, nothing can stop a person who is willing to pay the price for success.

—Winda Lingerfelt, Secure Financial Group, Inc., Brentwood, TN

Once I began reading the book, I couldn't put it down. So much that I read it a second and third time! With each read, I found the book more captivating. It's an inspiration for any entrepreneur and a manual for any business that is certain to change your outlook and approach to success. The book and Randall Baskin have had such a profound impact on me personally and professionally. My company has achieved goals that I never dreamed possible. I plan to make the book a mandatory read for my management team. This is simply the most powerful and uplifting book I've ever read. From the changes I've made in my company to my newfound faith and my belief in the power of prayer, my life will be forever enriched.

—Bobby Price, Founder, CEO and President, Price's Collision Centers

Randall Baskin's book is the perfect motivational read for any insurance agent needing to understand what it takes to succeed in the business. It is an entertaining and emotional true story that is very easy to relate to. Mr. Baskin has lived the American dream and truly knows what it takes to succeed and the heartaches that come along with success. I started in the insurance business in early 2012 and was lucky enough to have the opportunity to read it. It gave me the tools and inspiration to hit the ground running. This book is one of the best sales books available. He has referenced many classic motivational authors and illustrated how he applied them to his life and became one of the greatest successes the insurance/sales world has ever seen.

—Ace Wilson, Farmers Insurance Agent, Franklin, TN

I just finished one of the greatest and most inspiring books I've ever read. Not only does it inspire me to think even bigger, but it also reminds me of how good that God has been to me. Randall, I believe that God has blessed you with so much because he knew that you would turn around and bless so many others that are in need. The Good Lord definitely had a plan for your life. I'm proud to call you my friend. You may not remember but it was you who gave me my first marketing opportunity back in 1986. You allowed me to go into Virginia and recruit agents for Bankers Fidelity. That one break helped change the direction of my career forever. I will always be indebted to you for having the confidence in me to allow me to do that.

I feel that everybody will be inspired by your life story. I think that all of our big hitters with AIMC should read and help get it out to their producers. It's motivating, inspiring and most importantly there area lot of us old timers who have witnessed these things taking place in your life

—Mike White, President and CEO of AIMC, LLC

Growing Rich is a very inspiring and informative work that shows everyone how to become successful and how to fulfill his or her purposes, dreams and desires. Author Randall Baskin is the hardest-working, kindest and most giving individual I have ever known. His philanthropy extends far beyond what most people realize and this book is another one of many ways he has chosen to give back.

—Marty Irby, President, The Tennessee Walking Horse Breeders' & Exhibitors' Association

GROWING RICH

SUCCESS IN BUSINESS, SUCCESS IN LIFE

RANDALL BASKIN

WITH ROB SIMBECK

Copyright © 2012 by Randall Baskin
ISBN 978-0-9883541-0-4

Growing Rich Success In Business Success In Life
First Printing, 2012

Autumn Crest Publishing
1612 Westgate Circle, Ste 117
Brentwood TN 37027-9128

www.growingrichbook.com

Printed in the United States of America

Success

It may look big - it may look heavy.

But you can't stop it when you apply its principles.
The scale will balance every time.

See Chapter 21 for details.

To Sadie,
who has been the wind
beneath my wings
throughout the journey.

Acknowledgements

I wish to express my gratitude to every person who has inspired me to do my best, and to offer special thanks to those who taught me the value of using my time wisely.

Among those who are deceased, I am very grateful to Jack Schooley for introducing me to the insurance business, to my son Randy, and to my brother Marion and Cecil Ryan for always being there to help.

A special thanks to all of the dedicated employees and agents of Continental Life Insurance Company and American Continental Insurance Company for their magnificent support and their contributions to my journey.

Finally, I would like to acknowledge and express my deepest gratitude to my wife Sadie for the many hours she spent waiting on me as I built my career in the insurance business. She is still the wind beneath my wings.

Contents

Preface

I was seventeen years old, a dirt-poor high school dropout living with my new bride in the room I shared with my little brother just the week before. I was working in a creamery in nearby Murfreesboro, bringing home $37 a week, hoping just to save enough to move out of my parents' run-down home. Lying in the dark in that tiny sagging bed, I could never have imagined what life held in store for me. How could I dream that I would one day own a company worth well over $100 million, have two condos on the beach, drive expensive automobiles, and stay in luxurious hotels? How could I dream that one day I would give away millions of dollars in hopes of helping others better their lives the way I'd been able to better mine? In rural Tennessee in the days during and after the Depression, dreams just didn't come that big.

This book is about the journey between those two places. I hope it will inspire you. I hope it will convince you to cast aside any doubts you have about your own ability to succeed or about how much you can achieve. I want it to convince you to believe that the future—your future—is limitless.

I am convinced that success is there for anyone who brings the right mind-set to the table. Success is not complicated. It takes a dream, it takes a plan, it takes hard work, and it takes motivation—a burning desire to be successful. As you will see, I drew a lifetime of inspiration from books and speakers dedicated to sharing the secrets of success and fulfillment. You will hear me talk about Napoleon Hill and Earl Nightingale, Frank Bettger and Zig Ziglar. They convinced me I could succeed, and I want to do for other people what they did for me.

Among the many lessons I've learned is that a lifetime is very, very short. But it is short for everyone. In the quest for success, for meaning, for growth and wisdom, time is the great equalizer. Someone else may have more talent, more energy, or more money, but no one has more time. It is the one commodity you and I and Bill Gates all have in exactly the same amount.

The secret to success is using that time wisely. Within the pages of this book, you will see how my journey taught me the lessons that enabled me to succeed in the world of business and, I hope, in life. It has been a very good life. It hasn't been without its terrible tragedies—my older son, my namesake, whose office was next to mine, was killed while still a young man—but God has been faithful and has been with me during the good times and the bad. I am grateful for the many, many blessings I have received, and I would like this book to be my attempt at sharing those blessings.

PART I
THE EARLY YEARS

CHAPTER 1

"You Get To Do Your Own Thinking, And You Get Both Checks"

*I was a hard worker,
and I knew I could learn
pretty much anything.*

It started with a newspaper ad. I was twenty-six and out of work, sitting at the kitchen table and reading the *Nashville Tennessean*. I had been laid off from the Ford glass plant in West Nashville for about a month. While I drew unemployment, I had fixed up and painted the house, and now, with a wife and son to support and bills to pay, I was staring at the want ads. This one said, "Make two hundred dollars a week taking orders." I had no idea what kind of business it was, but $200 was a lot of money in 1958. Besides, I was a hard worker, and I knew I could learn pretty much anything. I had worked my way up from the factory floor to an office job at Avco, an aviation assembly plant where I'd worked before Ford, and I was ready for a challenge. The ad said to contact Jack T. Schooley, and it gave a phone number.

Two hours later, I was sitting outside his office, waiting for him to finish up with someone. There were only two things I didn't want to do—drive a truck and sell insurance. My dad had friends in trucking who were gone all the time and never seemed to earn much money, and Old Man Oakley had pretty much soured me on insurance. He lived about a half mile from our old home place when I was a kid, and he came by once a month to collect premiums on the debit life insurance policy he'd sold my parents. We had very little money, and now and then my mother had to put him off. He would talk pretty rough to her when that happened, and I developed a bad image of the insurance business.

Finally the office door opened, and the secretary sent me in. Jack Schooley was five-three or so, with a big potbelly that hung over his belt when he sat. He had sandy hair and a long face with a light freckled complexion and eyes that danced when he talked. He was well dressed, with a nice sport coat and a tie that arced over that big belly. He asked me where I'd worked and what I'd done, and then he leaned up across his desk and looked me in the eye, waving his hands and laughing as he made his points. He was a charming guy.

"So," he said, "when you're working at Ford, how much do you bring home?"

"About eighty-nine dollars a week."

"You work for that, don't you?"

"Yeah," I said.

He got out a blank sheet of paper and wrote

"89" on it. Beside that he wrote "work."

"The boss that you report to," he said, "how much would you estimate he earns?"

"I don't know," I told him.

"Well, what would you say? Two hundred?"

I said, "I imagine that's about what he earns."

"You work for this," he said, pointing at the "89." Then he wrote "200" under the "89." "The guy who tells you what to do and does your thinking for you earns two hundred. He tells you what time to start to work, what time to go to lunch, and when you can go to the restroom. Then he tells you what time you can go home, right? In other words, he does all your thinking for you."

"Well, yeah, pretty much," I said.

"Do you need somebody to tell you what time to quit work? Can't you think to do that?"

"Yeah, I can," I said.

He leaned forward even farther.

"Do you need someone to tell you what time to go to lunch? Can't you make those decisions yourself?"

"Yeah."

"Well, I'm offering you the same kind of job, but you get to do your own thinking." He paused a moment. "And you get both checks."

He wrote "289," and he circled it. It was great psychology. It was hard to believe I could earn that kind of money, but I kept picturing him handing me two checks instead of one. He'd convinced me, and I didn't even know what the job was.

Then he told me. It was selling insurance. My heart sank, although not as much as it would have before he'd given me his pitch. He said that it was just a matter of talking to people, of introducing them to a good product, and that

I'd have brochures and promotional materials. I thought back to the one thing I'd ever done that resembled selling. When I was still on the floor at Avco, maybe thirty of the one hundred people in my department were members of the Machinists Union. I got interested and signed up and then thought if it was good enough for me, everybody ought to be in it, so I started signing people up. I really had to stay on some of them to convince them it was a good move, but one by one they joined the union. Finally I had everybody in the department signed up except for one man, and nobody on earth could have convinced him. People in the union were so impressed they made me a committeeman. I thought about that campaign and figured, *If I can sell the union to those hard-nosed guys I worked with, I can probably sell insurance.* I told Mr. Schooley I'd take it.

"Be here at 8:30 on Monday morning," he said, "and let's put you to work."

Man, I thought as I left, I'm going to get both checks.

That weekend, I took my wife, Sadie, and eight-year-old son, Randy, to my sister Juanita's house in Murfreesboro for Sunday dinner. We were sitting around their big dining room table with her husband, Lynn, and her kids, who were fifteen and ten, talking and laughing, when I brought up my appointment with Jack Schooley. I told them I was going to start selling insurance the next morning.

Juanita laughed like she'd never heard anything so funny.

"You?" she said. "Sell insurance? You can't even talk plain! How are you going to sell insurance?"

I could feel my face redden. There were certain words I'd always had trouble pronouncing, so I wasn't really much of a speaker. I didn't think it was bad enough to be a problem, but she assured me it was. Then Sadie chimed in. She didn't like the idea of me working on commission, saying I'd be better off waiting for the glass plant to call me back. At least that was steady income.

I felt all the wind go out of me, and by the time we left Juanita's, I'd been talked out of the insurance business. It had been a nice thought, but there was no point thinking I was cut out to be a salesman. That Monday morning, I stayed home.

CHAPTER 2

Growing Up

*Those were the darkest days
of the Depression,
and there was never much money.*

I was born in the spring of 1932 in a cabin on my grandfather's property. It was a few miles west of Murfreesboro, Tennessee, and it looked like the place on the cover of William Young's The Shack, only a lot more run-down. Four years later we moved three miles down Highway 96 to the 108-acre farm that holds my first real memories. Land was cheap, and somehow my dad, who turned fifty-four that year, had scraped together enough for a down payment. The house, like the one on my grandfather's place, had no plumbing or electricity, and it had a cedar shake roof you could see daylight through until my dad had it covered with tin. When it rained, we set out pots and pans on the uneven linoleum floors to catch the water.

Those were the darkest days of the Depression, and there was never much money. We earned a little from the twenty or twenty-five acres we planted in cotton and corn, so I spent a lot of time walking behind mules and horses, plowing or laying off those long, long rows. All of us worked in the fields, and in the fall someone would drive the truck into town to pick up ten or fifteen day laborers, usually African Americans, to help us pick the cotton. Some of them were terrific at it, grabbing those bolls with both hands and stuffing several hundred pounds into their sacks over the course of a day. I never could pick very fast, and seventy or eighty pounds meant a good day for me.

We had a vegetable garden that covered more than an acre, and what we didn't eat, my mother canned. That and the two or three hogs we slaughtered every fall helped us get through the winter. The county had a food subsidy program that helped a lot too. We could buy inexpensive dried beans, brown sugar, and prunes—I remember eating a lot of those—one day a week, and there were a few items we could get for free.

We had seven or eight milking cows that needed tending every morning and night. At first it was me, my older sister, Betty, and my mother looking after them, and then as my younger brother, Baby, got a little older, he and I would do the milking and pump water from the well into the nearby trough the cows and horses drank from. Then we'd take the milk cans down to the front gate, and the milkman would come by and pick them up around 9:00 a.m.

The well sat down in a sinkhole, and we had to pump as gently as we could to keep the water from getting even muddier than it was. I don't know how we lived drinking that murky brown stuff. Eventually we had a well dug right behind the house; it was sulfur water and we didn't like it, but we drank it and left the old well to the animals.

We kept a milk can in a big tub of water in

the house to keep it cool, and every night in the flickering light of oil lamps, we'd wash our feet in the tub before we went to bed, since we went barefoot until it got pretty cold in the fall. Saturday night we'd take a full bath. My brother used to say that during the week we'd wash down as far as possible and up as far as possible, and on the weekend we'd wash our possible.

My dad, Arthur John Baskin, was taller than Little Jimmy Dickens, but not by much. Pop was a likeable guy who'd give you anything he had—it's just that he never had much. He avoided physical labor whenever he could. My mother, a high-tempered woman who was his height but twice his size, did a lot more work in the fields than he ever did. He'd help round up the cattle, but he always said he couldn't milk, and he never did. He'd do a little of this and a little of that, but shovels and hoes just didn't seem to fit his hands very well. He wasn't handy either. If something couldn't be fixed with baling wire, it stayed broke.

Pop didn't drive, but he owned a ton-and-a-half GMC truck, and he'd ride sometimes with our cousin Dave Baskin to a place in Murfreesboro that brokered deliveries. He and Dave would pick up cattle or feed or anything else that would fit in the truck and deliver it, usually locally but sometimes as far away as Athens, Georgia, for a little extra cash.

Dad also used that truck to earn some money just before Christmas. The rocky limestone soil of Middle Tennessee is perfect for cedar trees, and they were everywhere around our place. Every December starting when I was eight, we'd cut a bunch of them that were eight or nine feet high and load them in the back of the truck. With the cattle gates on the side, we could stack them pretty high, and I'll bet we got fifty or sixty trees in there. Pop would jump in the passenger seat, Dave would drive, and my brother Baby and I would squeeze in between them. We'd roll down Highway 96 on our way to Nashville, where we'd see a likely looking neighborhood and stop. We'd pull a few trees off the back and stand them up to show them off. We'd knock on doors and try to convince people to come out and look at our trees. It was my first experience going door-to-door, and it was exciting. I'd look for ways to get people interested enough to come see what we had.

"Two dollars for the little ones, three dollars for the bigger ones," Pop would tell them. We'd get pretty good crowds sometimes, and then when we'd sold what we could, we'd drive off and do it again. When we were done, Pop would divide up the money, and Marion and I could end up with ten or even twenty bucks as our share. Mom would see to it that we bought clothes or something else we really needed, and the rest of the money would help get us through Christmas.

One year as we were cutting trees I ran across a big one and decided I liked the looks of it. I figured it was my chance to bring in a little more money for us. It must have been twelve feet tall, but I cut it down and we dragged it to the truck. We spent the day going to house after house, and when we were almost out of trees, that thing was still sitting back there. I just hadn't thought about the fact that no one had ceilings that high. Nobody wanted to buy it. I was starting to get pretty depressed until finally a guy said he wanted it. It turned out he was a pastor who thought it would look nice in his church. He gave us five dollars for it, and I smiled all the way home.

There was one year when, for whatever reason, we just didn't do that well. Finally, late in the day, we stopped at a little family grocery store. Dad was a great horse trader—had to be, I guess, since we had so little money. He jumped out of the truck and started talking to the guy who owned the place. Dad said we'd trade the trees we had left for things we wanted—especially apples, oranges, and bananas—and he could resell them. In a few minutes, they'd struck up a deal.

The one real talent Pop had, and one of the few things he actually liked to do, was doctoring horses. He got known for being able to treat fistula, an abscess that can give them sores on their withers. Someone would bring him a horse, and he'd keep it a week or ten days. Early every morning he'd tie it to a tree and take an old knife and run through a routine that involved scraping the sore and rubbing blue medicine on it, passing that knife just so many times over the wound in what looked to us kids like hocus-pocus. The medicine probably healed the fistula, but the showmanship sold the service.

Mom and Pop didn't get along all that well, and it was worse when Pop drank, which he did at least once or twice a week. He bought from a bootlegger in Arrington when he could get a ride, and it made Mom furious when he spent what little money we had on booze. He'd always hide his bottles, usually near one of the cedars that ran in a row in front of the house. She'd search like a hound dog when she knew he'd left one out there, and more often than not she found it and poured it out.

Pop was a lot more likeable than she was, so I was more partial to him growing up, but as I got older I realized that without her we probably wouldn't have had anything. Her life was built around that house and farm, and she had the drive and determination Pop lacked. I got my persistence from her. She would do anything that needed to be done around the place, and she'd do anything in the world for her kids. She worked in the fields, cooked our meals, and saved every penny she could get her hands on. Our clothes may have been patched, but she made sure they were clean, and she made sure all five of us kids had new shoes and maybe new overalls in the fall. But it was obvious to all of us, even then, that she had psychological problems. I don't know much about either of my parents' childhoods, but apparently hers had been unhappy. She was born Virginia Anderson and raised on top of Monteagle Mountain in Sewanee. Pop was twenty-three years older than she was, and their marriage never seemed to make her feel happy or settled.

Mom couldn't control her temper at all. Pop would get to drinking, and she'd pick big fights with him, yelling and cussing and threatening. He was a happy drunk, but finally she'd provoke him to where he was yelling and cussing back and then they'd be throwing cups at each other across the kitchen table. Our neighbor Archie Macon would stand at the edge of his property just listening to them fight. Since I never knew when it might start up, I stopped bringing my friends around. I was ashamed of my parents and didn't want them to see what we saw all the time.

We kids tended to take Pop's side because he was easygoing even when he drank and she was so hard-nosed and bitter about it. After they'd been at it for a while and she saw the way we felt, she'd get to feeling sorry for herself. The mood would take hold of her and drag her down until finally she'd dig through the drawer for the butcher knife and threaten to cut her own throat. It happened time after time.

"I'm just gonna kill myself!" she'd yell. Eventually the only one of us who bought into it was Juanita, the oldest girl. She'd get upset and beg and plead with Mom not to do it, and a lot of times she'd actually wrestle with her, trying to get the knife away. It seemed like that only fed the behavior. In fact, if Juanita wasn't there, Mom was much less likely to do it. As I got a little older, I'd say, "Juanita, let her alone! Let her do it if she wants to!" knowing it was all a bluff, just drama cooked up for attention and sympathy. Knowing I didn't buy into it really made her even madder.

Mom used the family get-togethers we had on the Fourth of July at nearby Sulphur Springs or in Sewanee as an excuse for more drama. Some little thing would happen just before the Fourth, and she'd get mad and say she wasn't going. She'd make us beg her and beg her until finally, just in time, she'd say, "Well, I'll go this time."

Mom never did scare me that much, and I talked back to her more than any of the other kids. Despite that, I felt sorry for her. I knew that underneath it all she wanted what was best for all of us. She just couldn't make herself treat us right when one of those tantrums took hold of her.

CHAPTER 3

The Salesman

*"You've got the whole world to gain
and absolutely nothing to lose by trying.
For goodness' sake, try."*

I spent that next Monday trying to shake off the thought of Jack Schooley and those two checks. I glanced half-heartedly at the classifieds again and began hoping the glass plant would call me back. Sadie had a point. There was nothing steady about a salesman's income.

At 3:15 that afternoon, the phone rang.

"What happened to you?" It was Jack Schooley.

"I've thought it over," I said, "and I'm not cut out to be a salesman."

"Well, how do you know?"

I told him I wasn't much of a speaker and didn't know if I had the personality for it. He answered every objection the same way: "How do you know?" Finally he said, "Son, I'm interested in you, or I wouldn't be calling. There's one person you don't want to cheat in this world, and that person is Randall Baskin." I could feel his charm and enthusiasm coming through the phone line. I could see that belly and picture him leaning forward on the desk, the phone against his ear. "You are about to cheat yourself out of the best years of your life," he said. "Be honest with yourself. You don't know that you can't do this because you haven't tried. You've got the whole world to gain and absolutely nothing to lose by trying. For goodness' sake, try."

I didn't say a thing. I was just listening.

"If you want to try," he said, "be in my office tomorrow morning at 8:30," and he hung up.

Maybe it was his ability as a salesman, or maybe it made sense to me that I really didn't have anything to lose. I knew he must have seen something in me, or he wouldn't have called. In spite of Sadie and Juanita, I was in his office on Nolensville Road the next morning, April 22, 1958, ready to go to work. And so many times through the years, I've wondered, *What if he hadn't thought enough of me to make that call?*

That first morning, Jack went through a brochure with me, pointing out the highlights of the policy I'd be selling. It was issued by Bankers Service Life out of Oklahoma City, the company he represented. He talked a bit about selling door-to-door, then said, "I'll be sending you out with two managers who can help break you in."

The next morning we were in McMinnville, a town of eight thousand about seventy-five miles southeast of Nashville. We checked into an old hotel downtown—the bathroom was at the end of the hall—and I went out with one of the trainers. After each call he'd talk about what he'd said and done. At the end of the day we met up with the third man back at the hotel. They got out the maps and showed me the area I'd be working by myself starting the next morning.

Bankers Service Life had just begun operations in Tennessee. I'd be offering people a health and accident policy, tailoring the amount to fit their needs and finances. My commission would be 30 percent of the first year's premium on each policy I sold. Jack got 5 percent in what's called an overwrite, and a couple of assistant managers each got 2 percent.

The company had placed an ad in small-town newspapers, and I carried a copy as I set out in my car the next morning. Wearing nice slacks, a dress shirt, and a sport jacket, I'd pull into a driveway, walk up on the porch, and knock.

"I'm Randall Baskin," I said. "We're conducting enrollment here in your county. Have you seen this ad?" Whether they had or hadn't, I had a conversation starter, and it was up to me to make the most of it. I didn't talk numbers or policy details. I talked about how much peace of mind they could have. I talked about what they had to lose. Then I told them that for a price starting at not much more than few dollars a week, they could have a card that would take care of their medical bills if they got sick or had an accident. The room, surgery, whatever they needed—it would all be taken care of.

I guess I had a knack for it. I was good at engaging people in conversation, and right from the first I was making sales. In fact, one afternoon that week one of the managers rode with me to see how I was doing it. By the end of the week I'd sold seven or eight policies, and the trainers hadn't sold but two or three between them. But the way I looked at it, I was used to working hard, and I had no more sense than to follow directions. I liked the guys who were training me, but I realized pretty quickly that they weren't all that good.

On Saturday morning, all ten of us in the region got together at the office to turn in our reports, talk about the week, and get a pep talk from Jack. The reports went to Jack's secretary, Ann Whitson, who sent them to the home office. When the other guys heard I'd beaten everybody my first week on the job, they said it was dumb luck. The only ones who didn't downplay it were Jack and the assistant managers, the people with overwrites. They hoped I'd keep it up. We got checks that day for what we'd sold, and mine was for a lot more than I ever earned at the Ford glass plant.

After we'd gone over the week, Jack talked about motivation and salesmanship. He said we needed to read and listen to things that would inspire us and help us to be better, as salesmen and as people. He mentioned *Think and Grow Rich* by Napoleon Hill. He said it was a wonderful book, full of great ideas and sure to bring out the best in us. "Buy a copy and read it," he said.

Then he pulled a record out of its sleeve and put it on a turntable. It scratched and popped for a few seconds, and then a man with a terrific deep voice began speaking. "I'd like to tell you about the strangest secret in the world," he said. It was a factual presentation about the small percentage of people who really succeed in life and a look at the reasons why. It was clear that Jack was really taken with the man, whose name was Earl Nightingale. I thought the record was okay, but I wasn't particularly moved one way or the other. I looked at my watch now and then until a little more than thirty minutes after it started, it was over.

The next week we went back to McMinnville, and I did even better. It took an awful lot of calls and conversations, but I sold a couple of policies a day, and by the end of the week I had a check bigger than the first one. Saturday came, and the guys chalked it up to beginner's luck again, only not quite as condescendingly as the week before. And then Jack played *The Strangest Secret* again.

Every week got a little better. I worked long hours and dealt with rain and heat, but I sold the dickens out of that policy. Then, seven weeks in, I came home one night to find my wife standing at the door. She handed me a telegram. The Ford glass plant was calling me back at the same hourly rate I'd been at before. She was all excited about it.

"I don't want to go back there," I said. "I'm earning more money than I ever did there or anywhere else, for that matter."

She was pretty adamant. She agreed with some of the other salesmen that I was just lucky and that pretty soon I'd come back down to earth.

"If it's really that easy," she said, "why isn't everybody in the insurance business?"

Pop thought going back was a good idea too. "That's one of the best jobs around here," he said. "A lot of people would love to work there, and not many who do would want to give it up. Besides, you know what you're earning there, and you're in out of the weather."

I talked to Jack and he tried to talk me into staying, but Sadie threw enough of a fit that I finally told her I'd go back to the glass plant.

I finished out the week for Jack and then the following Monday went back to my job at Ford. I was an inspector, examining windshields that came rolling down a conveyor belt. I'd look each one over and use chalk to mark any bad spots or places that needed polishing. A few would have to be scrapped altogether. One after another they came down that line, and it wasn't long before it started to get to me. I couldn't help but feel like I was wasting my time. That weekend, I got out my records and calculated the average of what I earned selling insurance. In seven weeks, I had more than doubled my take-home pay. I went to Sadie and showed her the figures.

"I can probably earn even more than this," I said.

She didn't like it, but she said, "I told you what I think. I'm not going to say any more. I'm going to leave it up to you."

So I sat there on that stool at Ford again on Monday, trying to talk myself into giving notice. Sadie and my dad had planted enough doubts in my head that I didn't do it. Tuesday I went back and forth about it too. Nobody thought I should leave Ford, but Jack hadn't been lying when he said I could earn good money. And if I'd earned that much in the first seven weeks, what were the possibilities?

On Wednesday, all of that was going through my head as I watched those windshields coming at me. I thought about the days, weeks, and years ahead. *Man, I thought, if I do this long enough, I'll get to be so dumb I won't be able to spell my name. Do I want to do this the rest of my life?*

I knew the answer. I looked around and saw my foreman and motioned for him to come over.

"I want to quit," I said, "but I want to work out whatever notice you need—a week, two weeks, whatever you need me to work."

"What are you going to do?" he said.

"I'm going to sell insurance."

"Insurance? Why are you doing that? Maybe you should think about it. You're in here on the ground floor. You've got high seniority. Look, I've got enough help that I could let you quit Friday, but think ahead and make sure that's what you want to do. I'll check back with you."

That gave me some more time to sit there and think until finally in a couple of hours he came back.

"My mind's made up," I said.

"Okay. I appreciate you giving me the notice. I'll let you go Friday. You'll have the best of recommendations, and if you ever want to come to work here again, I'll take you back."

The next Monday I went back to Bankers Service Life. This time, it was for good.

Chapter 4

My First Goal

"Where did you get that money, boy?"

Of my four siblings, I was always closest to Baby, who was two years younger than me. Mom named him Marion Gene, but Pop never liked the name Marion—he thought it sounded like a girl's name—so he called him Baby, and that's the name that stuck. He was an easygoing kid, and mostly we got along pretty well. I had some of my mother in me, though, and I could be high-tempered. When we did get into it, I'd pop him on the nose, and anytime it started bleeding I knew Mom was going to get the razor strap and whip my butt. It didn't happen often, but it was often enough that she got to be really good at it.

I was still young when the oldest, Junior—Arthur John Junior—got married and left home, so I didn't see much of him growing up. Juanita was next, and she was working from the time I was young, although she didn't share anything with the rest of us. She had her own shelf in the icebox, and we weren't supposed to touch it, which was like waving a red flag in front of a bull. We'd see something in there and just have to have a little, which would make her really mad. Betty was just the opposite. From the first days she worked, she'd help the rest of us. Betty was smart and hard working, and she loved riding horses. Pop gave her the nickname Good Thing, and it was clear she was his favorite.

Summers we were outside most of the time. We didn't have many toys, but we were good at improvising. We'd play hide-and-seek or Annie Over, which involved throwing a ball over the house. We might take the top off a pan in the kitchen and use it as a steering wheel, pretending we were driving a truck. Between us, we might have a little toy truck to play with in the dirt or a toy gun to help us act out the Westerns we saw now and then at the movie theater. When the family went into town on Saturdays, Baby and I would always keep a sharp lookout as we rolled by the Princess Theater, where Ruby Baskin, a cousin's wife, worked as a ticket taker. When she was there, our folks would let us out. Baby and I, and sometimes Betty, would run to the ticket window with our quarters and slide them to her. She'd give each of us a ticket and push a button that gave us two dimes and a nickel each, letting us in for free. I realized later that she felt sorry for us.

Nobody celebrated birthdays. I don't remember a present or a piece of cake for anybody in all the years I lived at home. I do remember when I was around nine having my eye on a bicycle that cost eighteen dollars. It was all I thought about for a while. I saved every penny I came across and looked for any way I could earn some money. I'd help Owen Lane, a friend of my dad's who hauled things in our truck, with odd chores, and he'd pay me a little. Pop and Betty both gave me a little change to help out, but I knew I had a long way to go. Then one day I was at the J. C. Penney store in Murfreesboro, walking up a set of steps that led to a partial second floor when I saw that someone had dropped five dollars. It was a big boost for my bicycle savings. Not long after that we went to visit Aunt Oxey in Chattanooga, and I was walking with Uncle Ike one Sunday morning. I was looking on the ground for matchbook boxes. Juanita saved them, trying to see how many different ones she could collect, and she didn't care if there were matches in them or not. I wandered off a little way from Uncle Ike, and down on a corner I found seven dollars just lying there. I couldn't believe it. Of course, Uncle Ike didn't believe it either.

"Where did you get that money, boy?" he asked me. He was sure I had done something wrong. "Show me where it was laying."

Given that kind of luck, it didn't take me more than three or four months to raise the eighteen dollars, and I bought the bicycle. Every chance I got, I would ride it the five miles to school rather than take the bus. To this day, when I read a book that talks about the power of visualizing what you want or what you're trying to achieve, I think of that bicycle and all the concentration I put into it.

Except for the Fourth of July, when we had family gatherings with big picnic lunches under the trees, there weren't many special days. At Christmas, we'd decorate an old cedar tree and hang our stockings by the chimney. Most years we'd get some fruit and nuts and maybe one toy. One year, though, Juanita said, "Let's hang the stockings over here so they won't sway in the chimney." We hung them over on the wall, and on Christmas morning, there wasn't anything in them.

"I guess Santa Claus didn't see them," she told us, and I realized she'd known that it was an especially bad year and there wasn't going to be anything.

On winter nights we'd sit in the main room, which had a fireplace and an oil lamp, and maybe play checkers or Chinese checkers. The bedrooms weren't heated at all, and right before we went to bed we'd stand as close to the fire as we could and get as warm as we could stand, then run barefoot to our rooms and jump in under so many quilts it was hard to roll over. There were lots of times when a glass of water you had by the bed would freeze during the night.

Baby and I shared a tiny room that you had to walk through to get to the one Juanita and Betty shared. Mom and Pop slept in the main room. You could walk from there through a door to the living room, which shared the fireplace, although we never used it unless we had company.

All through the year, there were plenty of chores besides milking, watering the cows, and working in the fields and garden. We carried water in buckets to the house. We collected eggs when we heard the hens cackle and always tried to get there before Old Bill, our dog, who loved eggs too. It was tricky because the hens might lay in the henhouse, but then again they might lay somewhere in the weeds. Finally Old Bill got so bad we had to keep him tied up.

We used a push mower to trim the spots in the yard that were flat and smooth enough, and we had a Lively Lad, a serrated blade in a wood frame you swung back and forth, to trim the rest. We never saw poisonous snakes, but there were enough of the others to convince us to keep the grass and weeds short. We had to cut a lot of wood in the fall for the fireplaces and year-round for the wood stove, and the boys helped Uncle Grover butcher hogs in the fall because Pop just wasn't good at that.

Mom was a really good cook. Every morning there'd be biscuits and enough gravy to float a battleship and, if we were lucky, a few eggs. We ate a lot of dried beans, but on Sundays one of us would run down a chicken and wring its neck, and we'd have it with potatoes and green beans or maybe sweet potatoes with marshmallows on top. We didn't waste a bit of it. We ate the feet and head and everything. Until I was grown, I thought everybody did. We ate a lot of sowbelly too. That big garden gave us plenty of tomatoes and cucumbers, green peas and butter beans, and cantaloupe and watermelon.

Whatever was left over after a meal would get covered up and sit on the table. That was okay until this old gray cat of mine learned how to take a claw and hook into the screen door and open it from the outside to get in. He'd come across the floor and jump up on the table and get into the leftovers.

I never even named that cat, but he had taken up with me and I was really fond of him. He'd sit on my lap all the time and want me to pet him. That didn't mean anything to Mom. Once he started getting into the leftovers she got aggravated and drove him all the way to Murfreesboro and put him out. I was heartbroken.

About a week later, we were sitting on the front porch, and I heard the screen door squeak and then bang shut. I ran in there, and the cat had come back all seven or eight miles. Even my mom was impressed, and she let me keep him after that.

The end of summer meant school, and I went to Kingwood School, which had two rooms—first through fourth grade and fifth through eighth. I remember in the early years that the Ryan girls, who were Juanita's age and older, looked after us when we caught the bus out on Highway 96, making sure we were okay and weren't getting picked on. As the weather got colder, the older boys built a fire when we got to school, and we'd gather around the big Franklin stove until it got warm.

One cold December morning when I was nine, the boys were talking loudly as they loaded the stove with wood. I can still remember seeing their breath as they talked about an attack on a place called Pearl Harbor. *Where in the world is that?* I wondered. It had happened the day before, but we didn't have a radio—we still didn't have electricity—so I hadn't heard a thing about it.

I was a B and C student. I liked arithmetic, science, and agriculture but never did particularly well in English. My parents didn't care much one way or the other. I think Pop finished high school, but I don't remember that either of them ever talked to one of my teachers. I guess they figured there wasn't much they could do about how well we did in school, so they just sent us and left it at that. We never had a book in the house besides our schoolbooks, not even a Bible. Once in a while there'd be a magazine somebody brought home. I never even liked comic books. In fact, I never read much of anything I didn't have to until I was in my twenties. I did take some inspiration from Pop's handwriting, which was really beautiful. I'd watch him sign his name, and he'd put in all sorts of swirls and loops. Junior had handwriting like that, and I guess I picked up a little bit of it.

I was in fourth grade when people started talking about electricity coming our way. The TVA had been building dams and running wire all through the Tennessee River Valley, and our turn was coming. We had wires strung in the house, and lamps and wall sockets put in. I couldn't believe what that house looked like all lit up the first time. Then we got a radio, and we'd all listen to the Grand Ole Opry on Saturday nights.

Two things happened during those days that have stayed with me all my life. The first involved the clothes people used to give us. I don't remember if it was an agency or just individuals, but I'll never forget one pair of big boxer shorts I had to wear under my school clothes, which were almost always overalls with patches on them. I can still see my skinny little legs in the big leg holes of those boxer shorts, and my mother pulling at the waist and pinning them to one side so they'd stay up. One day at school my pants split open, and all the kids saw those big old pinned-over shorts I was wearing underneath. I was embarrassed to death.

Then, when I was about eleven, my sister Betty was earning thirteen dollars a week at a drugstore. She was only sixteen or so, but she took it upon herself to give me and Baby seventy-five cents each on Monday morning. We took that to school to pay for the week's lunches. Now and then Betty wouldn't be at home, and we'd have to go to school empty-handed. It was awful because my teacher would always embarrass us in front of the class, saying, "You know you're supposed to have that money in here Monday morning," and she would just go on and on about it.

One Monday, Betty had spent the weekend with friends and wasn't at home. I couldn't face the prospect of having my teacher humiliate us again, and I told my mother I wasn't going. As we argued about it, Baby went on ahead toward the bus stop. Mom finally made me go, and so I started walking, head down, spirit broken, across the fields that led to the highway. About halfway across, I just fell down onto the dirt, crying. I beat my fists on the ground and kicked in sheer frustration and dread. I cried until finally I couldn't cry anymore, and then I got up, dried my tears, and went on and faced it.

I have relived that experience a thousand times in my mind, and I look back on it as one of the best things that ever happened to me. That and those awful hand-me-down boxer shorts made me decide that I didn't want to be poor for the rest of my life. It made me vow that I would always provide for my family. It made me determined to make it in this world, and it made me willing to work hard enough to do it.

I never set out to be rich, but because of that morning and the way I felt, I set out not to be poor.

Chapter 5

Determined
To Make It

"By the way," I'd say,
"who do you carry
your health insurance with?"

I went back to the insurance business determined to show everyone what I could do. Most of the people in my life thought I was making a mistake, but I had never known anything that gave back to me what I gave to it as quickly as selling insurance, and I was ready to give it everything I had.

I picked up where I left off. I guess I was just a natural, and I worked hard to get better. I made it a point to dress well, and more than one person said I looked a little like Billy Graham walking up the sidewalk, only with a briefcase instead of a Bible. I knew how to look people in the eye and show them I was interested in them as people, and then the small talk always led to insurance talk that focused on their lives, their needs, and ultimately their fears. I would talk with them about how important it was that their families keep what they had worked so hard to earn.

"If something were to happen to you," I would ask, "would your family be able to get by?"

Getting the chance to talk to people wasn't difficult. They expected the occasional door-to-door salesman in those days, and country folks were generally friendly and unafraid. Few people worried about strangers or locked their doors.

Sometimes the company would do a mail-out asking people who were interested to mail in a card. That gave the salesmen good leads, but it got pretty expensive for the company, so they would pay you a car allowance of up to fifty dollars if you got out and dug up business yourself. I always selected that option because I liked the extra money and because it gave me some great basic training I never would have gotten otherwise. I had to learn to start from scratch, engage a person, and work up to a sales pitch.

One of my favorite ways of working was looking for someone. I would walk up on a porch and knock, and when the person came out, I'd pull out a lead card that had a name and address on it. Sometimes the name and address were real. Sometimes I'd made them up.

"I'm trying to find Sarah Johnson, who must live somewhere nearby," I'd say. "Do you know Mrs. Johnson?"

"Why, yes," she might say. "She lives down the road about half a mile." Sometimes she would holler in to her husband to ask if he knew. In any case, people were always nice, wanting to help me find whoever I was looking for. There was nothing threatening or pushy about someone just asking directions. In fact, they were generally a little curious about who I was and what I was selling.

The woman might walk out on the porch to talk for a minute. The whole time I'd be selling myself, which is the key to sales. I'd thank her two or three times, and then as I started to leave, I'd stop, as though I'd just had a thought.

"By the way," I'd say, "who do you carry your health insurance with?"

By this time, she felt like she knew me a little. She wasn't under the gun. She saw that I was just curious, and she might tell me about the coverage they had—or didn't have.

"Ma'am," I'd say, "let me show you something. You need to see what I've got here."

If she hesitated, I'd say, "Now, I know you can't tell me you're not going to buy because you haven't seen it yet." And I was off and running. She'd almost always be willing to talk for a minute or set up an appointment when her husband came home. I'd show her my plan and tell her the advantages it had over what they had now. To me, that was about the easiest way in the world to sell.

I remember once when I was making sales like crazy and hadn't gotten to the person I was looking for. "I hope I don't ever find him," I told the girl in the office.

I learned early on not to think about the commission. I had to focus on what I could do for the customer. What was the finest plan of protection I could give this person based on what he or she could afford? Of course, I had to know our product. I also had to know our competition's products, and I knew them by heart. I could quote the waiting period and the limitations and exclusions of most of our big competitors.

I   was   selling   variations   on   a   single

hospitalization policy that Bankers Service Life offered. It would pay anywhere from six to thirty dollars a day on a hospital room and so much toward surgery and other health expenses. I didn't want to show people something that was beyond their budget, so I learned to gauge their financial situation by looking closely at the neighborhood, their home, their car, and their furnishings. A good, solid policy might carry seventy or eighty dollars a year in premiums; I always felt that if I sold a policy that cost more than one hundred dollars a year, I was in high cotton. If they already had insurance, I'd tell them what I could do to better their coverage, but in those days, most people in the areas we were working—probably 60 percent or so—didn't have it. In 1940, only 10 percent of Americans had health insurance. By 1960, it was 75 percent, but a lot of the rest were in rural areas like those we were working. Some of them were easy sales. Some were almost impossible. Most were somewhere in the middle. This was an era when the insurance industry was judged to have integrity and a good product at a reasonable cost, and that helped those of us selling it.

Sometimes the other salesmen would meet for lunch, but if I ran into any of them, it was accidental. I'd stop at a country store and get a piece of bologna or cheese and some crackers and then get back at it. I was there to sell insurance, and I was always out working until the last porch light went out. If Friday night came and I didn't think I'd sold what I should, I'd work Saturday. It didn't happen often, but if I needed that boost, I was more than willing to put in the extra time.

I learned to ask for referrals, and that always

opened the doors a little wider. Someone would tell me, "You might want to talk to my cousin Bobby, who lives a couple of miles down the road." Then when I talked to Bobby, I could say, "Your cousin Ruth just bought a policy, and she said you might be interested in one."

At night at the hotel we'd share the names of anyone prominent we'd sold because that was always a great selling tool.

"By the way," I'd say at one point during my pitch, "did you know that Mr. So-and-So has a policy with us?"

We called them chiefs and Indians, and you always wanted to mention any chiefs you'd sold in that community. I sold one and didn't even know it at first. A Mrs. Alfred Marks bought a nice policy from me, and a couple of days later someone told me she was Al Gore Sr.'s sister. Al was a United States senator at the time and one of the biggest names in Tennessee. Carthage, where we were working, was his hometown, and he had a big, fine home there. You can bet we all told people she had one of our policies after that.

When I'd been selling for a while, I became a trainer myself, taking new guys out. One of them was my brother Baby—now that he was an adult we were finally calling him Marion—who came back from the service that summer and wanted to try his luck at selling insurance. He went on calls with me and watched what I did. I explained the policy and talked about selling and then let him give it a try. He would talk to customers and bring them to the point where I knew they were ready to sign up, but he'd talk right through the opportunity. He never could see when to close. He'd miss it every time, and I'd have to jump in and try to pull it back.

Finally I decided just to sit there and let him lose one he should have had. Then when we got back in the car and started down the road, I went over the entire discussion, point by point. "When you were at that point," I said, "you were close. Then when she asked you that question, that was selling time. Anytime they ask you a question, it's a buying sign. That's when you should move right in."

We sat there on that country road rehashing it for an hour until I finally started to get through to him. After that, he began to catch on, although when he went out on his own, he'd still call me to close a lot of times and we'd split the commission. I worked harder training him than anyone else I ever worked with. Normally a new salesman would catch on in a couple of weeks. It took six months until Marion was good enough and confident enough to go out and close by himself.

Once, while he was still new, I was working in Lebanon, Tennessee, and I wasn't having a very good week. Sadie was helping Marion and his wife—he had married Sadie's sister—move into an apartment in Murfreesboro. I drove over from Lebanon to Murfreesboro, and he and I went down to the Dairy Queen to get a hamburger at about 9:30 that night. The girl came over to wait on us, and through the little screen door, I said, "Young lady, I want to ask you something. Who handles your group insurance?"

She just looked at me.

I said, "Don't y'all have insurance?"

"No."

"You don't have any kind of coverage?"

"No."

I said, "Unlock the back door and let me come in. I need to show you something."

She unlocked the door, and I got my briefcase. I sold the two young ladies a policy right then and there. This was on a Friday night, and if I hadn't made those two sales I would have had to work Saturday.

Weeks when it was slow were pretty rare for me, but there were times when I'd get down. No matter how long you've been at it or how successful you are, now and then rejection gets the best of you. I had to learn to come back from that, to turn my attitude around and go from negative to positive, because staying positive is the key.

Early on, nice houses could intimidate me. It may have had something to do with where and how I grew up. One day I was working out near Lebanon, and I turned in the driveway of a great big colonial home with big pillars out front. I stopped there and thought, *I'll bet they've got more insurance than I've got.* So I backed up and turned around and drove off.

I hadn't gone a hundred yards when Jack's question from that first phone call came into my head: *How do I know that?* I slammed my foot on the brake and stopped, put it in reverse, and went back to that house. A sweet elderly lady came to the door and invited me in. I ended up selling her two nice plans. I was about to leave when I heard someone walking in another part of the house. I said, "Does someone live here with you?"

"Oh, they live on the other side of the house," she said. "That's Mr. Jackson and his family. He takes care of the farm and milks the cows and all that. Come on."

She introduced me to him, but he had to go milk, so I made an appointment to come back an hour and a half later and made another nice sale to him. That became one more experience I could look back on and draw confidence from when negative thinking got the best of me.

Chapter 6

The Love Of My Life

*"I met this girl last night
that I'm really hung up on."*

Despite all the problems my parents had, I'd have to say I was usually pretty happy growing up. Most of the kids I knew were in the same boat we were in when it came to money—none of us had much. There were a few families who had nice cars and were obviously doing well, but in school everybody was pretty much the same. The kids with money were nice enough and usually didn't look down on the rest of us.

Scouting was another place where differences didn't matter—all of us wore the same uniform and learned the same skills and ideals—and it was one of my favorite parts of growing up.

I had seen other Scouts when I was younger and set my sights on joining. When I was thirteen, I got the chance, becoming part of Troop 103 in Murfreesboro. I saved up for my uniform the way I had for my bicycle, and I was so proud when I put it on each week. Mother or one of my sisters would drive me to the meetings, which were held in a church basement. It was the only real outside activity I had as a kid, and I really looked forward to it.

Our Scoutmaster was a popular local life insurance executive, a very nice man named Tommy Martin, and I soaked up all the things he and our handbook taught us: leadership, citizenship, fitness, practical skills like knot-tying, woodworking, and first aid, and virtues like hard work, courtesy, and thrift. I really studied that handbook, wanting to be prepared for each new lesson. I was pretty good at most of it, but I remember having a world of trouble rubbing two sticks together to start a fire. I tried it several times and never could get it to work. The Scout sign and salute, both made by putting the first three fingers of the right hand together, were tough for me because my fingers were short and I guess a little crooked. I always had to push my fingers together with my left hand.

I was part of Scouting for two or three years, and I still regard it as one of the best influences in my childhood. The Scout motto, "Be Prepared," was something I've carried with me all through life and is something I still talk about.

Starting with ninth grade, I went to Eagleville High School, riding the bus like I had to Kingwood. I enjoyed it, although I wasn't any better as a student. As much as I liked arithmetic, I didn't like algebra, and English was still a struggle. I really enjoyed shop. I liked working with my hands, making things like birdhouses. I joined the basketball team, but I wasn't all that good, and I never did get to play much. My parents felt about sports like they did about school in general; they never came to a game.

I was fifteen or so when we kids started attending church regularly. We had some friends who were going to a new little church called Green

Hill Baptist over on Burnt Knob near Almaville. On Sunday mornings we'd get on the church bus and ride over with them. I had never thought much about religion as a kid; we just weren't a religious family. Now and then I had gone to the Methodist church with my friends the Ryan boys, but it didn't go much further than that. This new church, though, had a preacher who was really good, and we felt more and more like we needed to make a profession of faith. We joined the church, and the preacher made arrangements for several of us to get baptized, taking us over to First Baptist in Murfreesboro, which was nice enough to let us use their baptismal pool.

I was also fifteen when I met Sadie Tucker. A friend of mine named Gene had a date with her, and he lined me up with another girl so we could double up. Something happened and the other girl couldn't make it, but I went along anyway. Sadie and I liked each other from the moment we met. I thought she was wonderful, and she always said it was love at first sight. We were supposed to go to a movie over in Smyrna, where she went to high school, but there wasn't much on so we went and got something to eat instead. By the end of the evening, Gene was just our chauffeur. I had pretty much taken his girl from him.

The next morning I was still so love struck I felt sick. I was cutting cedar for a guy, but when I showed up at his place I couldn't concentrate at all. I just lay down in the woods and thought about Sadie.

"What's wrong with you?" he asked.

"I met this girl last night that I'm really hung up on. I never had a date like that."

He just laughed.

Finally I told him, "Look, you don't have to pay me today. I don't feel like working," and I went on home.

From then on, I spent as much time with Sadie as I could. As soon as I turned sixteen, I got a license and bought a '34 Plymouth coupe, which made it a lot easier to see her. If I had money, I'd take her somewhere, and if I didn't, I'd just go over to her house, which was about twenty miles away.

The car wasn't much. It wouldn't start unless you pushed it and popped it into gear. Usually Marion had to help me do it, so I'd take him along when I went to Sadie's. She had a younger sister named Dot, which made him a lot more willing to go. They later started dating and eventually got married, and I always felt responsible for that.

The four of us would sit in the living room talking, and at 10:00, Dot would get up and go to bed. Marion would lie down on the couch and go to sleep. I'd keep talking to Sadie, and eventually Mr. Tucker would say to his wife, "Sarah, what time is it?" loud enough so I could hear him. That's when I knew it was time for me to get my behind out the door. I'd have the car on a little hill, and Marion would help me push it off. I'd stop and get fifty cents worth of gas, which would get me home. I'd put fifty cents more in it before I went over the next time.

The car finally died, and when it did, I went to Juanita. She had always looked out for herself first, but when I asked if she would help me buy a car, she said she would. She put six hundred dollars up front, and we bought an old Pontiac. We agreed that we'd own the car together and that I'd pay her my half in installments. We also agreed that if something went wrong while she was driving it, she was responsible, and if something went wrong while I had it, I was responsible. Well, the first time she went off with it, something happened to the transmission, and she wanted out of the deal right then and there. She just gave me the car and then started dunning me for the money—all six hundred dollars. Every time she saw me she brought it up, and every time she did I told her I didn't have any money.

"Juanita," I said, "I can't pay you because I don't have it, but I promise you one thing. I promise you will see every penny." Eventually she backed off a little, and as soon as I had the money, I paid her for the car.

The summer I was sixteen I got a job at the Wilson Creamery on West Main Street in Murfreesboro. I worked from seven to four making American cheese in a big vat. We'd cook the whey, stirring it until curds formed. We'd drain the excess liquid, then work and turn the cheese and drain it again. What started as twenty inches of liquid would wind up as four inches or so of cheese. We'd drain the last of the liquid, then run it through a cutter. We'd put those chunks into buckets, pack them down with our fists, and salt them. We put presses on them overnight, and then they would go into a cooler.

It was hot, hard work. We had to take salt tablets because we'd sweat so much, and all of the guys would throw a handful of salt into this liquid called "starter," a bacterial culture used to start the process that curdled the milk, and then they'd drink it. It took me a while before I'd try it, but when I did, I thought it was good. It had an unusual taste, like buttermilk but even richer.

Between Sadie and work, school didn't seem very interesting. When I was seventeen and we'd been going together two years or so, she and I decided to get married, and I dropped out of school. I was earning all of thirty-seven dollars a week at the creamery, and I guess I figured we could live on love. Both our parents were okay with it, and Sadie's aunts threw a little shower for her. I took my paycheck, and she and I went up to Franklin, Kentucky, with Juanita. We found a preacher and got married, and I used my last five dollars to pay him.

That night, Betty and Juanita let me and Sadie sleep in their bedroom, which was bigger than the one Baby and I shared. That was our honeymoon. With nowhere else to go, we moved into my old room, which Betty and Juanita still had to walk through to get to theirs. Marion slept on the couch.

My mother was as unpredictable as ever. She'd throw a tantrum now and then that would turn everything upside down. One night Sadie and I were taking a bath out of a wash pan in our room, and my mother decided she wanted in.

"We're taking a bath," I said.

"Well, open the door."

"We're taking a bath!"

She was all wound up and determined to get in, and she reared back and rammed her shoulder into the door and knocked it clean off its hinges and onto the floor, with Sadie and me both naked.

After just three months or so we decided we had to get out, and we moved into her parents' place. From the beginning, I didn't feel welcome there. Her mother didn't think I'd amount to much, and now and then she'd say so. It was always a little tense there, and Sadie and I would have little fights. I still had some of my mother's temper, and when we did fight, I'd get in the car and drive off. Finally one night her mother let me have it, telling me that Sadie was welcome there but I wasn't and that I might just as well go back home. I don't know that I'd ever felt as low as I did that night. We had no privacy and hardly any money, and I felt like I had nowhere to go. I sat on the porch of her parents' place and cried.

I was going to have to make some changes. Sadie was pregnant. I had a family, and I was going to have to support it. If I was going to better myself and improve our situation, I would need another job. I hadn't finished high school, let alone college, so it was going to have to be manual labor. I left the creamery and found a job working nights with the Lane Chest Company, milling panels the company used to make cedar chests.

Then I decided I had to find a way to get us our own place. I couldn't even think about buying a house at the time, but surely I could find a beat-up old trailer and set it up somewhere on Dad's land. Sadie and I drove to Nashville in that Pontiac, which had started smoking badly every time we drove it, and stopped at a lot to look at trailers. The cheapest thing we could find had a price tag of $425, and even that was way out of reach. I told the salesman we couldn't afford it, and Sadie started crying. She cried all the way home.

Chapter 7

Nightingale and Hill Change My Life

People with goals succeed because they know where they're going

Jack Schooley's Saturday-morning sales meetings were everything a hungry young salesman could have asked for. There were always eight or ten of us, and after we turned in our reports, Jack delivered a pep talk sprinkled with practical advice. He might speak about decisions or enthusiasm or effort. Then he'd go straight to motivation.

"You know what you sold this week and what you're averaging," he'd say. "Now, I want you to set a goal for yourself for the coming week. Make it a goal you really have to reach for because that's what it takes to keep improving. Now, write it down on a piece of paper. Along with that goal I want you to write this: 'A winner never quits and a quitter never wins.' It's to remind you to keep going no matter what, to believe in yourself and keep on working."

We'd each write down our goal and that slogan on a piece of paper.

"Now stick that in the pocket where you keep your change," he'd say. "Then every time you put your hand in your pocket, it will remind you of your goal."

Then he'd play us that Earl Nightingale speech. He did it every week. At first I was still looking at my watch, doing the math to see when the record would finish, but now and then I'd hear something that really struck a chord.

"People with goals succeed because they know where they're going," Nightingale said at one point. "Failures, on the other hand, believe that their lives are shaped...by exterior forces." That just resonated with me. I could shape my destiny if I believed enough and worked hard enough. I could turn the number on that piece of paper in my pocket into reality. In fact, I was proving that already.

The next week something else on the Nightingale record would resonate with me, and I'd have another motivational tool to work with. As I saw how I could apply the things Nightingale said to what I was doing, which was presenting people with a way to protect themselves should disaster strike, I got a little stronger, a little smarter, a little better at my job. Soon I was listening eagerly to The Strangest Secret from start to finish, over and over. I borrowed Jack's copy, took it home, and taped it onto a four-track cartridge, brand-new technology that let me listen to it in my car, something I began doing a lot. It opened up my world. I grabbed especially onto his statement that if I just applied the basic principles diligently, success was automatic. It was going to come.

I couldn't even begin to guess how many times I've listened to that record and the tapes I made of it over the years, but even in my last years as president of my own company, I'll bet I was listening to it thirty or forty times a year.

Jack also talked a lot about Napoleon Hill's Think and Grow Rich, a book that outlined principles of personal development that had brought great success to a number of people. I bought a copy and was lifted up and inspired by it. I applied the principles to my life and they were every bit as useful as those on Earl Nightingale's record. The chapter on faith may be the single most inspirational thing I've ever come across. To this day, anytime I'm down, I read this:

> *I fully realize that no wealth or position can long endure unless built upon truth and justice. Therefore I will engage in no transaction which does not benefit all whom it affects. I will succeed by attracting to myself the forces I wish to use, and the cooperation of other people. I will induce others to serve me because of my willingness to serve others. I will eliminate hatred, envy, jealousy, selfishness and cynicism by developing love for all humanity because I know that a negative attitude towards others can never bring me success. I will cause others to believe in me, because I will believe in them, and in myself. I will sign my name to this formula, commit it to memory and repeat it aloud once a day, with full faith that it will gradually influence my thoughts and actions so that I will become a self-reliant and successful person.* *

---

* *Excerpt from* Think and Grow Rich, *by Napoleon Hill, is used with the consent of the Napoleon Hill Foundation. Information about the Foundation can be found at www.naphill.org.*

I can't tell you how much that impressed me and how motivational it was. Those lines made me want to be successful, and to be successful the right way. Just reading them boosted my self-confidence. I was sitting in my easy chair at home the first time I read that, and I laid back right there and started memorizing it. I began saying it out loud every day. There's something so powerful about those words, and they never failed to lift me up when I was down, to give me purpose when I lacked it. I credit a lot of my success to the fact that I recited that out loud every morning on my way to work. I can still quote it more than fifty years later, and to this day it means a great deal to me. It keeps my soul alert to the importance of doing the right thing because it's the right thing to do.

Hill and Nightingale led me to a lifelong appreciation for inspirational literature. I was always reading something motivational, whether it was Dale Carnegie, Norman Vincent Peale, or Frank Bettger and then Zig Ziglar and Robert Schuller. Those books were rooted in real stories about real people, and the bottom line was always the same—Believe. Believe in yourself, in the good you can do with your life as well as with your product or service. Strive for greatness. Set goals, be persistent, and serve others, and success is inevitable. It is a message so simple and straightforward that the average person doesn't get it. Somehow I did, taking it in until it was a part of me.

I was determined to succeed. From the time I got married I had a burning desire to have a nice home and a nice automobile, and I was willing to work to make it happen. I don't know if I've ever met a man who worked as hard as I did and was as determined as I was to make it. It helped that the insurance business was so direct. The harder I worked, the larger my checks were.

During my first months with the company, they gave us a book of premiums, items we could win if we sold so much insurance through the summer. I saw a nice stereo system and decided I wanted to win it. I thought I'd be lucky to get it by the first of the year, but week in and week out I met my goals and piled up the points. By August, I had enough to order the stereo, and before the end of the year, I won a pair of big speakers to go with it.

I still have that stereo. For years I kept it in the reception area of Continental Life, the insurance company I founded in 1983. It symbolizes the first real goal I ever set that came out of what I was learning from Napoleon Hill and Earl Nightingale. I exceeded that goal, and from then until now, I've exceeded every goal I've ever set.

They also had a "Salesman of the Month" award, a laminated plastic wall plaque. I remember taking my first one home to our place on Ennis Road and hanging it on an empty wall. I stood back and looked at it and said to Sadie, "I'm going to cover the wall with these." And through the years, I did just that.

That was about the time Sadie really started coming around. She wasn't crazy about all the hours I was putting in during the week, and I remember one time when my brother came home pretty early and he and Dot went out to dinner. When I got home, much later, Sadie was sitting on the porch, good and angry. After she'd gotten some of it out of her system, I sat down beside her and opened my briefcase. I showed her what I had sold just since four o'clock that afternoon. I told her about what it took to set up those appointments and the commitment of time involved, and then I showed her what I had earned that week. Seeing how much I had earned really made an impression on her. It was one of the best and smartest presentations I ever made, and it helped get Sadie on board. The stereo, the plaques, and the checks I kept bringing home did the rest.

I still remember my own feelings at the time. Sometimes on my way to Woodbury or McMinnville I would pass the Avco factory where I had worked. I had a spot where I'd pull off and look over at that old plant. Many a time I sat there in my car picturing my old buddies who were still there, hot, sweaty, and dirty, doing all the things I used to do. As much as I appreciated them and their hard work, I would give a little prayer of thanks that I had risen above that and was now managing my own time, like Jack said I could, doing something I enjoyed a lot more that was a lot better for me.

At my other jobs, I'd been living from week to week. That wasn't the case anymore, and it was time to learn how to manage what I was earning. Jack helped there too. I was working in Lawrenceburg and staying at the Lawrence County Hotel when he brought me my first renewal check, which was my share of our customers' premium renewals. It was for seventy-five dollars, and it was over and above the straight-commission front money we got every Saturday. Jack sat down and said, "I know that you're earning more money than you've ever earned in your life, and this check is like getting money from home that you didn't write for. You're going to get one every month, and I know you don't need this to live on."

He paused and let that sink in.

"You know, to be successful," he said, "you have to reverse the interest process. Instead of paying interest, you need to receive interest. To do that, you have to save first. Take this money, and go down and open a savings account."

He wrote down "savings account," and I still remember what beautiful penmanship he had. The letters swirled and flowed like my dad's.

"This is not an ordinary account. This is a very special account." He started writing again. "It's a no-touch account. Now, don't worry about what you're gonna do with it. It'll take care of itself. Next month you're going to get another one of these checks. It's going to be a little bit bigger. You take it and put it with this. This will work for you twenty-four hours a day, when you're awake and while you sleep."

That first conversation went in one ear and out the other, sort of like the Earl Nightingale record did at first. My second renewal check, a month later, was for $103. I hadn't even cashed the first one—it was still in my billfold—but I realized Jack was onto something. This may be a good idea, I said to myself, and I went down to Fidelity Federal on Nolensville Road and opened an account.

Jack was a brilliant man and a great motivator. He got me started on the road to self-improvement, and the lessons he shared still mean a lot to me. He thought a lot of me too. The girl in the office once told me, "I get so tired of hearing, 'Randall Baskin. Randall Baskin.' Every time Jack interviews somebody he buzzes me and has me bring your records in so he can show them the kind of money you can earn."

That was extra motivation for me. I wanted to keep my sales figures high enough that Jack would want to keep showing them off. It was one more reason to work hard, and in turn that work kept coming back to me in the form of more sales and higher commissions. I had been outselling everybody since the beginning, and now there were weeks when I was selling more than five or six other agents put together. I always looked at it as having no more sense than to do exactly what Jack said to do.

He certainly had a way of making all of his lessons memorable.

"I just happen to have an opening for a manager," he'd say to an agent, and if you hadn't heard that before, it really got your attention.

"Fred," he'd say, "I want you to start with Fred. You manage him well. You see that he gets started early in the morning, and I know you'll do that because I believe you're a good manager. See that he acts enthusiastic. See that he makes that last call at the end of the day. See that he does a full day's work five days a week. Manage him. Manage him well, and then when he becomes successful— and I know he will because I know you're going to be a good manager—then I'll give you another man and you can manage him and help him to do the same thing you've been able to do with Fred."

Jack was such a good motivator that I wanted to make every week good just to please him. I was a puppet, and he pulled the strings. The entire time I worked for him, I wanted to do well by him.

Chapter 8

A Trailer and A Son

*"There comes a time when you've got to
stand on your own two feet."*

I was determined to find a place that Sadie and
I and the baby we were expecting could call our
own, and I decided to talk to Mr. Clendenon at
the Bank of College Grove. He had given me two
small loans, one for car repairs and another that
let me catch up on some bills. Pop had cosigned
both, and I'd paid them back on time, so I figured
it wouldn't hurt to ask. I went to his office and
told him about the $425 trailer. We filled out the
paperwork, and he counted out the money to me.

"I'll get my dad to sign the papers," I said.

"Son," he said, "you won't have your dad with
you forever. There comes a time when you've got
to stand on your own two feet. I believe you'll pay
me back." That was the first time anyone really
trusted me on my own, and I was determined to
pay back every nickel on time.

Sadie and I drove to Nashville, bought the
trailer, and hitched it to the Pontiac. We drove back
to my dad's place, with that car smoking the whole

way, unhitched the trailer, and set it up in the front yard. As beat-up as it was, we were happy. We were finally out on our own.

It would be hard to do justice to how old and decrepit that trailer was. It was all of twenty feet long, and the door wasn't five-and-a-half feet high, so I had to duck to go in and out. The roof had a rotten canvas-like cover, and the first time it rained we had leaks everywhere. We put pans out to catch the water, and the next day I climbed up on the roof and spread black roof tar on the cracks, patching as best I could. Then, after the sun beat down on it for a while, it would crack, and the leaks would start all over again. From then on, I was up there patching every couple of months.

We saved a little bit every week toward the bills we'd have when the baby was born. Finally, on December 3, 1949, we got in that old Pontiac and drove over to the Rutherford County Hospital in Murfreesboro, where Dr. Lois Kennedy delivered a baby boy we named Randall Ray Baskin Jr. Sadie and I were as happy as we could be.

I was working from 5:00 p.m. until 2:00 a.m. at Lane Chest in the glue room's 130-degree heat. To this day I'm not sure how I stood it. I'd reach up, pull a board down, and put it on a conveyor where it would run across the glue. I'd put a second board on top, even them up, then tighten them down, and run them through a heater that dried the glue. Those two pieces made up part of the top of a chest. We had production quotas, and if you beat yours, you got a small incentive bonus. I was fast enough that I could stay ahead of my boards and help the other guy working alongside me. After the shift I'd catch a ride—I always left the car at home in case Sadie needed it—and get home at 3:15, as tired as I could be. I'd walk across a couple of fields toward our little old trailer and look for the light. If it was on, my heart would sink a little because I knew Randy was sick again. He was sick a lot as a toddler. Sadie would be up rocking him, trying to comfort him. He had these spells where he would cry and look like he was holding his breath, and then he would have spasms that would make him go limp. He'd fall down sometimes, and I was sure he was going to hurt himself.

We took him to Dr. Kennedy, who didn't know what was wrong with him. The spells went on, and time after time I'd come home in the middle of the night, see that light on, and know it was bad again. We went back to Dr. Kennedy off and on for months, and finally when Randy was about eighteen months old, Dr. Kennedy made an appointment for us at a free clinic run by Vanderbilt University Hospital. The place was jammed with people, and it took two days of waiting and seeing people before they finally did all the blood tests they wanted. They told us he didn't have enough of something or other in his blood, and they gave us a bottle of red medicine. I'm not sure what was in it, but after we gave him that medicine, he never had another spell.

When Randy was about two, Sadie and I hitched up the trailer again and moved to a trailer park in Smyrna so I could be closer to Lane Chest. There was a nice big Airstream parked near the entrance, and every time we went in or out, I thought about how I'd give almost anything to live in something that luxurious, especially since we still couldn't keep the water out. I'll never forget one stormy night when the ceiling started leaking right above us just as we went to sleep on the pullout couch that served as our bed. As it dripped onto us, we got up, put a pan out to catch the water, and walked to the other end of the trailer. There were two seats in the kitchen that faced each other and you could put a board between them and rearrange the cushions to make a bed. We made that up and crawled in and then, just as I was getting settled, lying on my back, a drop of water hit me almost square between the eyes. It was the first time we had to move twice to get a good night's sleep, and it was pretty depressing.

I was always looking for ways to earn a little extra money. I wanted more than anything to give my family a good life—I still remembered that vow I made when I was a kid—and I wanted Randy to have it better than I did. Lane Chest would buy all the cedar I could cut, and there was still a lot of it around. On weekends and on my days off I'd cut for Frank Prater, who lived across the main road from Mom and Pop's place. He always bragged on me as being a good worker. No matter how hot it was, and it gets plenty hot in the summer in Middle Tennessee, I could always work harder than anybody. In those days, I could pick up a cedar log a foot thick and seven or eight feet long and carry it out onto the road where they'd load the truck.

At one point Pop and I were talking about the cedars around the property, and he said I could have them if I wanted to cut and sell them. There was one especially big tree out back that had the fence nailed to it. It took a while, but I chopped it down and then, as I stood on the trunk, which was sitting four or five feet off the ground, trimming branches off, the axe glanced off a limb and the blade went through the heel of my shoe and into my foot. It was bad enough that I had to go to Murfreesboro to get it sewn up before I could come back and finish my work. I got all the cedar cut and sold, but by the time I got the doctor bill paid, my part of the proceeds didn't amount to much— and I still have the scar.

I kept looking for ways to better our life. Sometimes it was small things, like getting a great price on a beautiful cedar chest, one of the fringe benefits of working at Lane Chest. It was one of the first really nice things we had, and through the years a lot of precious and valuable items went in there, starting with my old Boy Scout handbook and all the love letters Sadie and I wrote to each other while we were dating.

Sometimes it was big things. My brother Art was working at the time for Avco Manufacturing, an aviation-related company with a plant in Nashville. I knew it offered higher pay and a better chance for advancement than I'd ever have at Lane Chest, and I was very happy when he got me a job there late in 1950.

Art served as a big motivator for me in those days. Working for Avco let me see close up how successful he was. He was a purchasing agent for the company, and I'd see him walking through the plant in a sport coat, white shirt, and tie. I was out there on the plant floor, using a compressor-driven rivet gun to assemble the tail sections of B-47 bombers, and I'd hear, "Art Baskin, call the operator," over the loudspeaker. I went home tired and dirty, while Art looked like a million dollars, helping to run the place and earning a lot of respect for what he did—not to mention the fact that he earned a lot more money than I did. I was very proud of him, but it made me want a job like his.

I made it my goal to start moving up the ladder, and I knew that to do that I'd need a high school diploma. I signed up for my last year of school through The American School, which provided a correspondence course, and got to work. I studied late at night and on weekends, filling out my lessons and mailing them in, on top of my forty-hour workweek, and when I finished, I received my diploma from Eagleville High School. I wanted to go somewhere in life, and this was another important step.

Chapter 9

After 3:15 On Friday

If you want to be happy,
you have to act happy,
so I started whistling.

Jack always instructed us to stop and analyze
our calls after we made them, and I formed the
habit of doing just that. "Ask yourself," he said,
"would you buy from that salesperson?" Whenever
the answer was no, I'd do what I had to in order
to change my approach. Sometimes I'd tell myself
to quit selling insurance and just start visiting
with people. I'd make up my mind to be the most
enthusiastic person they had ever met, and then
in the end I'd get around to talking to them about
insurance. That always seemed to work for me.

During that first year, five or six of us spent a
lot of time in Smith County, about an hour east of
Nashville. We'd been there for three or four months
and had worked it from one end to the other, selling
a lot of insurance. When we'd done all we could
do there, my brother and I moved on to Jackson
County. It was next door to Smith County, and we
figured it would be just as good. It wasn't. Jackson

County was up in the hills, and it was home to a
different breed of people. They were poorer, and they
looked at us differently. I always wondered if they
thought we were revenue agents on the lookout for
moonshine. By Thursday night, I had earned about
thirty dollars, and Marion had earned maybe sixty
dollars. We decided to go back to Smith County to
work Friday, then go home. When we got back to
Smith County, though, Marion said, "I've had all of
it I want. I'm going home." I said, "Come on. Let's
make a day of it. You're already here."

"No. You can if you want," he said. "I'm going
home."

I decided I needed to stay and keep working.
I was generally full of confidence, and I could be
vocal about it, so I'd been running my mouth a
little. I had been talking to a lot of people who were
in or who had been in the insurance business, and
I heard the same thing from a lot of them: "You have
your good days and bad days, your good weeks and
bad weeks."

"Correction," I said. "You have your good weeks
and your great ones. There ain't no such thing as
a bad week. Maybe a bad salesman."

I wanted to prove I could put my money where
my mouth was, but that Friday wasn't any better
than Monday through Thursday. I'd had a few
slow weeks but never anything close to this bad.
At 3:15, with thirty bucks to show for a full week's
work, I pulled my car over to the side of the road
and said, "Randall Baskin, you need to face the
facts. This is your first bad week in the insurance
business. Go on home, have a good weekend, and
make up for it next week."

Somehow, though, that thought didn't sit right
with me. Jack Schooley always said, "When you

make a decision, analyze it. Is it the right decision? What's going to happen if I do this?" So I looked at the situation. *If I go home now, I thought, I'm not going to have a good weekend. I'm going to be ill with the wife. If I stay here, I probably won't sell anything more, but I don't know that for sure. If I go home now, I KNOW I'm not going to sell anything. Surely to goodness if I've worked this hard, I can stay here and work until it starts getting dark. So I decided, I'm going to stay here. I'm going to do the best I can and see people until it gets dark.*

I needed some enthusiasm, and I figured the best thing to do was to pretend I had it. If you want to be happy, you have to act happy, so I started whistling. It's hard to be down when you're whistling—try it sometime. I whistled as I walked up to the first house and knocked on the door. No one was home, but I whistled as I walked back down the steps and got in the car. I drove to the next house, went in, and made a real nice sale, and afterward I asked for a referral as I always did by then. The old fellow pushed back his cap, scratched his head, and said, "I'll tell you where you can probably make a sale. We were playing checkers down at the store one night, and this old boy who lives right there next to it said something about needing to get some insurance. You might talk to him."

I went down and sold the guy two good policies, and I sold his mother two as well. At that point, I was just one sale short of qualifying for some of that expense money, and as I drove home, I thought about Tom Napier, who ran Napier's Cafe outside of Carthage. I'd be passing right by his place. He had promised to buy something when his current insurance came up for renewal in three months.

He was the only prospect I had, so I wheeled in there about 8:00 and said, "Tom, I know I'm early, but I need one more sale today. I might come back three months from now, and you won't be home. I'll check with your neighbor, and he'll say, 'Well, he's up there in Smith County Hospital.' And you know the policy you've got now isn't all that good. So I decided I'd just come on and get you in force now. You don't have to pay it by the year. You can pay it quarterly or whichever way you want to."

"How much did you say that was?" he said. I looked it up and told him, and he bought it. I entered it in my ledger book, where I logged every sale I made, listing the policy number, address, and all the rest, and called it a week.

The next morning, I was at the meeting in Jack's office filling out my report when my brother walked in.

"Well," he said, "I guess you knocked 'em dead, didn't you?"

I set the paperwork on the table and showed him what I had done. I had turned that $30 week into about a $250 week. I never again had a week even close to that slow, and I look back on that turnaround as something I made happen. It was by no means my best week ever, but I always called it that because I did it all after 3:15 on a Friday and it showed me what was possible. I was so thankful I stayed there and pulled it out because it gave me another level of confidence that I carried with me from then on. And it gave me a whistling habit that served me pretty well too.

Chapter 10

Our First Home

"Art," he said, "I want you to watch that young man. He's going to go places."

About the time I went to work for Avco, Mom and Pop realized that with all the kids gone, the farm was just too much for them. They knew it wouldn't be long before they'd sell the place and buy a home in Murfreesboro. First, though, Pop offered me eight acres as sort of an inheritance while they were still living. It was just down the road from the house in the middle of a big thicket. There was no way even to see the highway from there. I spent every spare minute clearing out brush and trees with an axe or a briar blade to make room for the trailer, with Pop helping now and then. Finally I got it cleared off enough so that Sadie and I could hitch the trailer to the car one more time and move back.

One of the things I remember from those days is she and I sitting together at night on the couch, taking turns reading aloud from the Bible. Sadie had been raised Church of Christ, but she had joined the Baptist church and gotten baptized. It took us a while, but we eventually read all the way through the Bible.

During the day, we spent a lot of time getting the place in shape. I was cutting brush and cleaning up one day when Art, his wife, Jean, and her granddaddy, Mr. Goodwin, drove up unexpectedly. It was raining lightly, and I was soaking wet when they got there. The place didn't look very good, and neither did I. I said, "Y'all go in. I'm so wet I can't." Jean went in and talked to Sadie for a few minutes, but they didn't stay long. Sadie and I were both pretty embarrassed about it, thinking we'd made a bad impression, but years later Art told me what Mr. Goodwin said when they left there. "Art," he said, "I want you to watch that young man. He's going to go places."

Once the brush was cleared, my spare time went into building a shed over the trailer to help stop the leaks. I built an outhouse, then started on a room attached to the front of the trailer, and when that one was done, I added another. I got us a couple of hogs and built a hogpen, cutting tall trees as poles and using a flat rock as a base. Finally I built a little shed that looked like a chicken house, built a stall inside, and got a milking cow.

Every morning before I went to Avco I'd get up and milk that old cow, and every now and then she'd decide she wasn't going to come into the stall. She'd go down into the bushes sort of like she was hiding, and I'd have to chase her and try to run her back up to the barn. One Saturday morning I ran after her for the longest time and just couldn't get to her. Finally I went back to the trailer and got my shotgun. I fired a shot in the air from behind her, but apparently it wasn't quite high enough and some of the pellets caught her in the tail and in the udder. She made a beeline and didn't stop until she was in that stall of hers. Then she sulked. I thought I'd killed her. I hadn't, but her bag got infected and I had to bathe it regularly with warm salt water. I milked her onto the ground for a good month or so because the milk was bloody before she finally healed up—but I never had any more problems getting her to go to the barn!

I worked as hard on that place as I did with everything else. One year I even tried to bring in a cotton crop. I had Sadie out there helping me chop cotton, although it didn't take long for her to let me know she wasn't cut out for that kind of work.

Despite everything I did to the place, I was always pretty much ashamed of it. I did realize that it was a great location. It sat up on a little hill and had a nice view of the road once it was all cleared off. I dreamed in those days of the big house I'd build on that section of Pop's property, and I vowed I'd work hard enough that some day Sadie and I would have a home we could be proud of.

Chapter 11

Because It's The Right Thing To Do

*Being honest and fair. . .
served me as well as
any natural ability I had.*

Being a door-to-door salesman exposed us to all kinds of people. Some were friendly; some weren't. Some were hard to get into a conversation, and others would talk all day if you let them. I learned that if you handled them right, they'd hardly ever be rude to you, and I found that my approach—I like to think of myself as Mr. Enthusiasm—really helped establish a good atmosphere.

I also learned that there was more to knocking on doors than business. I was gaining a glimpse into the lives of real people, and it couldn't help but affect me. I remember very clearly calling on a family in Hartsville, Tennessee. They had a fifteen-year-old girl who wasn't more than three feet high. She looked like a five- or six-year-old. Her kidneys had never developed, and her parents told me she probably had six months to live. When I left, I couldn't get her out of my mind. The family didn't have much, and they were facing a tragedy they could see coming at them like a slow-moving train. I was doing really well for the first time in my life, and my insides told me I needed to do something to make their lives just a little better. The next morning I went back to Hartsville. I went in a ten-cent store and bought a whole bunch of things I thought that little girl might like, and took them out there and left them.

That little girl's memory stayed with me, and I think she fanned a spark of giving inside me that has never gone out.

On the other hand, every now and then there could be a real temptation. Once when I was going door-to-door in Readyville, just outside Woodbury, a middle-aged woman invited me in. We were talking about insurance when her daughter, who was about nineteen or twenty, walked into the room. She was really pretty, and her mama introduced me to her. From that point on, she'd sort of wander in and out as her mama and I talked.

"You're a very good-looking guy," her mama said to me, "and my daughter's a very pretty girl. Maybe y'all might like to go to the show or something."

I was wearing my wedding ring, but neither one of them cared a bit. I could hear the girl in the other room with a baby—it was obvious she'd gotten pregnant and wasn't married, and now she and her mama were looking for someone to take care of her and that baby.

"Well," I said, standing up after a few minutes, "I've got some other calls to make, and I'd better be going."

"You can come back anytime, you know," her mama said.

That conversation crossed my mind again the

next day. It was a real temptation—probably the biggest one I ever faced—but I just didn't let the devil get hold of me. I knew I had no business going back there, and I've always thanked the Good Master for giving me strength enough not to do it.

I was good at keeping my focus. My job was to learn and pick up every advantage I could. Insurance gave back, and I knew my potential was limited only by my willingness to work.

Having a door opener like a newspaper ad I could refer to or a "chief" I could mention always helped, and I learned quickly to ask for testimonials. Once, early on, I got a copy of a large claim check that had gone through for Hugh Hackett, who lived outside Carthage. He'd been a hard, hard sell, and I knew he'd make for a good letter of recommendation now that we'd paid some big hospital bills for him. I went looking for him but couldn't find him. Before long, another claim check went through. He'd been in the hospital again. Finally I learned that he'd died and that his widow had moved into Carthage. A neighbor told me where she lived, and I went to visit her. When she saw me, she came out of that door and hugged me.

"I don't know what I would have done if it hadn't been for you," she said. She praised the company and told me how good we'd been to her husband and how promptly we'd paid the bills. "If I can ever do anything for you, you just ask me."

"You can," I said, "right now."

"You just tell me what it is."

"Have you got a tablet?"

"Yes," she said.

"I want you to write me a letter and tell me in that letter what you just told me in person."

She sat down and wrote it all out and handed it to me. For the longest time I carried that letter door-to-door, showing people what a real customer, someone right there in their county, thought about the company and our service. I carried it until it started coming apart, and then I taped it up and carried it some more. Eventually I had to photocopy it and carry the copy.

Other customers sent in letters praising us, and I always carried at least one to show to potential customers. The closer the person lived to the person you were selling, the more effective it was, but all of them helped a lot through the years.

I loved hearing good things from customers. There were times, after I was in management and didn't go into the field anymore, that policyholders would drive for an hour or more into Nashville to show me a policy someone else was trying to sell them and see what I thought about it because we'd been good to them and they trusted me. Of course, I'd just sell them a better plan. They knew the kind of service that I, and the companies I represented, gave, and they wanted to do business with us. Those customers provided me with lessons I carried all through my career. They also helped me build a great business.

Bankers Service Life was new in Tennessee, so when I went into an area, I had to visit local hospitals to make sure they would accept the policy. After I'd been selling for about a year, I took some claim forms to one of them. The lady got up from her desk, walked around, and said, "I'm gonna shake your hand. I had never heard of your company until you were in here a year ago, and now just about every other person that comes in has got one of their policies. You must have really sold some insurance."

I smiled and said, "I did all right." It was a good feeling because I knew the people who bought it had a good policy. On most points we were stronger than the competition. We had no waiting period. We paid promptly. The one thing I considered a drawback was that Bankers Service Life did not have guaranteed renewal. Everything was renewable at the option of the company. I never did see where they terminated anybody, but they had the contractual right to do so.

Once, after I'd made a sale, written up the policy, gotten it signed, and accepted the check, the man said, "You hear about companies canceling these policies. Can this one be canceled?"

I thought about a book I'd been reading—I think it was *How I Raised Myself from Failure* to *Success in Selling.* The author, Frank Bettger, said that when you're hemmed in the corner, the way to get out is to tell the truth. Not a half-truth, but the bold truth, without hesitating. If you hesitate, you lose. I looked the man straight in the eye and said, "Yes, it can be canceled. If you've been honest with me, I don't think they will cancel. If you haven't been honest with me on something, I think they would cancel you. But they give you more coverage for less money than you'd get with a guaranteed renewable because you're not paying for the people who abuse it."

"Well," he said, "you've been truthful with me. I'll be truthful with you. I went to the doctor the other day with the wife, and he put her on little white pills for high blood pressure. What about that?"

I picked up his policy. "Let's put that on the application," I said. "They won't ever cover that, but if you had not told me, they could have gotten out of most any claim, even if it was unconnected to this, because you falsified the application. Now you'll still have a quality policy."

I hadn't been in the business very long, but I was always so thankful I read that book. Tell the bold truth. I made that sale. They issued the policy, excluding the high blood pressure, and both of us came out all right.

Being honest and fair, doing what was right because it was the right thing to do, served me as well as any natural ability I had. That went back to something Pop used to say all the time. He didn't teach me a whole lot, but he'd say, "Do the right thing, and treat your fellow man like you want to be treated." I wanted to be a salesman, but I didn't want any of the negatives associated with the profession. I didn't want to make a sale unless I believed in the product and knew it would pay if people needed it.

At the same time, I learned that being a salesman is being an actor. It's a craft, with scripts to learn and cues to follow. I could start from any conversation about the weather or the neighborhood or a front-yard flower bed and get quickly to talking about protecting what they'd earned if something went wrong. My brother would tell jokes as he talked to people, staying lighthearted all through his presentation, but I was always a very sincere and serious salesperson. Once I really had their attention, I'd let my voice go high and low like a preacher's. I'd get into the middle of a hard sale, and I'd be full of confidence, knowing I was going to sell them. It was fun to watch it unfold.

"You know, Mrs. Jones," I'd say, "a good doctor can almost tell who has insurance and who doesn't by the expression on their faces. Now, when you lie down in that hospital bed, counting those spots on the ceiling, you're either going to have insurance or you aren't, and then is not the time to decide. You can't buy insurance on your house when it's on fire, and you can't buy health insurance once you're in the hospital."

I'd show her a chart. "Your chances of losing the value of this home are four times greater with a doctor bill or a hospital bill than because of your house burning down. You wouldn't want to take a risk of not having insurance on your house, and I don't blame you. But what's more important—you or the house? You've got to really stop and think. You've got to be realistic and get coverage where it's needed the most. Don't you agree?"

She'd shake her head in agreement, and I'd be one step closer. At this point she hadn't said she was going to buy. If a customer says she'll take it, you hand her the pen, but most people never say they'll take it. I'd be filling out the form as I asked questions—address, age, place of employment. I'd make an X to show her where to sign and hand her the form on a clipboard with the pen on top. Now she had a filled-out policy and a pen in her hand, and more than likely I had a sale.

Chapter 12

Nashville

It was a big step up for us—
it was our first experience
with indoor plumbing!

When Randy was six months old, Sadie took a job as a sales clerk with J. C. Penney in Murfreesboro. Every morning she caught a ride into town on the milk truck, and I'd pick her up in the evening. For a while, a neighbor kept Randy during the day, and then Sadie's grandmother, Jessie Mae Fly, moved in with us and took care of Randy while we worked. She slept on the couch in the front room we'd built on to the trailer, and having her there made that tiny place seem that much smaller.

I rode to Avco with Fred Maxwell. He took five of us who lived in the Franklin Road/Almaville area with him in his station wagon. We'd pay him so much a week for gas, and I'd leave my car at his place or drive to one of the others' homes and ride with them to his place.

After three or four months, Sadie took a job with Third National Bank in Nashville. At 6:15 a.m., she'd catch a ride with a friend to Murfreesboro, then board the bus to Nashville, walking several blocks from the bus station to the bank's main office at the corner of Church and Fourth. I'd get home from Avco about 5:45 in the evening, then drive the eight miles to Murfreesboro at 8:00 to pick up Sadie—it took the bus that long to get there. It was tough on both of us, and it just couldn't last. We realized we needed to move to Nashville to be closer to work.

So, in the spring of 1951, we started looking at places in Nashville, and we found an upstairs apartment at 927 Acklen Avenue. It was up a very steep flight of stairs at the back of the house, and as summer came, it was pretty warm inside because we only had a window fan, but it was a big step up for us—it was our first experience with indoor plumbing! To be able to get into a bathtub full of hot water was a real treat for both of us. What was even better was that our landlord, Mrs. Cochran, kept Randy while we worked.

Sadie took the city bus to work, but at least now it was just a few miles, and occasionally she could catch a ride with someone in the neighborhood who worked downtown. We were just another happy young couple with a baby at the time, and we dreamed of owning a home. After we'd been on Acklen for a little over two years, we started looking at houses and found one at 2724 Ennis Road. It was on the south side of town, not too far from Avco and across the street from my older brother Art and his family. We paid $8,300 for it, and we were really excited about moving into our first actual home. I rented a U-Haul truck, and Marion helped me load it. We hadn't rented a dolly, and when we finally got to the refrigerator, Marion decided he would take the lower end as we went down that steep flight of stairs. He got the corner set on the first step, but when we tipped it again to move it to the second, we lost control, and Marion rode that refrigerator all the way down the steps, catching his hand between it and a large drainpipe that ran from the upstairs bathroom along the wall. We had to stop right there and take him to the hospital to get his hand sewn up, which cost me my last eighty dollars.

Once we'd moved to Ennis Road, Sadie drove to the bank, although she had to park five or six blocks away and walk the rest of the way, since we couldn't afford the high parking rates near the bank. Before long, though, she found a better-paying job much closer to home at Ferro Fiberglass Company. That was about the time that Marion and Sadie's sister Dot got married. Art helped Marion get a job at Avco, and he and Dot moved in with us for a while until they bought a house on Evelyn Street, about a mile from us.

We were really proud of our house, and I decided I would like to have a basement, so I went out back and started digging next to the foundation. After work and on weekends, Marion would come over and dig with me. Each time we cleared enough dirt we would install a steel post anchored in concrete to hold up that section of the house and then dig out the concrete blocks that had been holding it up. Several people advised me that I was making a big mistake doing it the way I was.

"That floor's going to sag," more than one person told me, but I figured if I was careful enough, that wouldn't happen.

We had a pick, two shovels, and a wheelbarrow. We dug a ramp, and whenever we filled a wheelbarrow with dirt, one of us would push it up the ramp while the other pulled on it with a rope attached to the front. We used the dirt to level the lower part of the yard. We poured concrete for the floor, dug a drain by hand, and installed pipe. We worked all summer until we'd completed the project, and by the time winter came, I had a nice basement. When I checked the floor, it was level, from one end to the other, which surprised everyone but me.

About that time, Sadie and several of the girls she worked with went to see a fortune-teller. I remember how aggravated I was that she would spend money on such a thing when we were trying to get ahead on seventy-five or eighty dollars a week.

"Don't you want to know what she told me?" she said. "She said there would be two children in our family and that something would happen to one of them. She also said you will become very successful—wealthy, in fact."

Randy was six and we hadn't decided to have another child, and as much as I wanted to get ahead, hard work was letting us pay the bills, but it sure wasn't making us rich. I didn't put much stock in either prediction, and I was still bothered about the money.

Mom and Pop sold their place in 1953 and bought one on East Lytle Street in Murfreesboro. They also looked around for jobs and found work at Central State Hospital for the Insane on Murfreesboro Road near Nashville. Pop, who was over seventy by then, became a general handyman, and Mom, who was in her late forties, became a nurse's aide, wearing a white uniform and working with the patients. The jobs came with a furnished room on the grounds of the hospital, and they took one so they wouldn't have to drive back and forth, although they kept the place on East Lytle and returned to it years later. I was glad they'd found the jobs because now they had some real security and stability.

There were even more changes. My sisters and Marion and I had talked them into joining us on Sunday mornings at Green Hill Baptist. Neither had ever been religious, but they started going and eventually they joined. Finally one day Juanita, Betty, Marion, and I went with Mom and Pop as they were baptized in Stewarts Creek, three or four miles from the church. There were fifteen or twenty other church members present and three or four other people who waded out into that creek with Mom and Pop. The preacher prayed with them and then guided them as they lay back into the water, went under, then came up, baptized. It was an emotional experience for all of us. We had really wanted them to be saved, and I was very pleased that they did it. After that, Mom went to church more often than Pop, who never seemed as committed to it, but I think it helped them both—they didn't cuss and raise hell nearly as much after that—although part of it was no doubt just them getting older.

Randy, meanwhile, was starting school. I was really glad he was a healthy boy, something I'd worried about during the days when he was so sickly as an infant. Jean Haley, who lived across the street from us, kept Randy sometimes while Sadie and I worked, and she had two boys of her own. The three of them played together a lot and even though both were a little older, Randy could always keep up with them. He loved skating, and Sadie would go with him when I was working late hours selling insurance. He loved swimming, too, and went to the lake a lot when the weather was nice, usually with Marion and Dot. Weekends were for family time, no matter how hard I worked during the week.

Randy wasn't as good when it came to school. He went to Whitsett Elementary School off Thompson Lane and really had a tough time there. Reading came hard for him. Sadie and I both worked with him, and I remember many nights and weekends sitting with him for hours trying to help him learn to read. I knew it was possible to do well in life without more than a high school education, but I really wanted to give him every advantage. I just wanted, as every parent does, for him to have a long and happy life.

Chapter 13

Agent Of The Year

*I didn't want to go through
that kind of nervousness again,
so I signed up for a Dale Carnegie course.*

One sale at a time, day in and day out, I kept
learning and improving. With just eight months
of work in 1958, I was named Agent of the Year
for bringing in more sales than anyone in the
company. That earned me an invitation to attend
the annual awards banquet in Oklahoma City. I
had to drive all the way to the Memphis airport to
catch a plane—the first one I ever boarded.

In my second year with Bankers Service Life, I
generated more in annualized premium payments
than any other single agent, and that earned me
another invitation to Oklahoma City. Phil White,
the company's agency director, had made several
trips to Tennessee and recognized my passion for
the business. He told me he wanted me to deliver a
speech on enthusiasm at the awards presentation.
My first thought was, I can't do that! I've never
made a speech in my life! But I felt like I couldn't
say no. A girl in the office had given me a copy of

Gleanings, a book by A. M. Burton, the founder of the Life and Casualty Insurance Company of Tennessee. It was really inspirational, and it helped give me the confidence that I could put something together. I wrote and memorized a speech, and I stood in the living room, practicing it several times in front of Sadie.

I arrived in Oklahoma City the day before the banquet and spent the entire night sweating and sleepless in a nice air-conditioned hotel room. By morning, I was a nervous wreck. I got dressed and went into the banquet hall, which had big round tables and a stage with a long head table and podium. I was second on the program. I was even more nervous sitting there on that stage, looking at a plate of eggs and bacon and then at all the people in the audience. I was sure the people at the table with me could hear my heart beat or see it pounding in my chest. I took one bite of egg and had a hard time swallowing it.

Well, no way I can do this, I thought. I'm just going to tell Phil I don't feel good. I went looking for him, but I never could find him. As I was walking around, the program started, and I went back to my seat, more nervous than ever. Phil got up and introduced George Kaiser, an agent from Missouri who was one of the company's best salesmen. I had to do something to get my mind off myself and my speech, so I focused on George. I guess the Good Master was taking care of me because as I listened to him speak, a calmness came over me. I relaxed enough to be able to think. I realized that I knew what to say—I had memorized my speech. There was no reason to panic.

George finished what turned out to be a very good talk, and when the applause died down, Phil

introduced me. I couldn't believe how calm I was.
My mind wasn't on me anymore. I gave my talk,
and before I knew it, I had come to the story I was
closing with, just something light I'd heard about
bravery turning to fear:

There was this football team made up of players
who were smaller than average. Their biggest
players might have weighed one hundred seventy-
five pounds or so. But they had enthusiasm, and
so they won game after game, making it all the
way to the play-offs. Well, the first team they faced
in the play-offs looked like giants compared to
them—we're talking two-hundred-fifty-pounders
up and down the line. The smaller team won the
toss, but on the kickoff, their return man was
flattened before he made it to the fifteen-yard line.
On the first play from scrimmage, their halfback
lost four yards. The coach sent in a message:
"Throw the ball to Bill," but the team tried another
handoff and lost five more yards. The coach sent
in another message: "I said throw the ball to Bill!"
That's when he heard a voice call out from the
huddle, "Bill says he doesn't want the ball!"

Everybody in the place laughed, and then they
stood up and applauded. It had gone really well,
and that standing ovation did wonders for me.
When I went back home, though, I realized that
there were going to be more speeches to give and
that I'd need help. I didn't want to go through that
kind of nervousness again, so I signed up for a
Dale Carnegie course. I took Sadie with me the first
night, and we met the area director, Buzz Busby,
who stood at the door and introduced himself to
all of us as we walked in.

"You're Randall Baskin? Hello, Randall Baskin.
You're Sadie Baskin? How are you, Sadie Baskin?"

He did that with everybody, and then when we all got seated, he said, "I'm going to attempt to call each one of you by name." There were about forty of us, and he walked down the row, calling one name after another. "You're Randall Baskin. You're Sadie Baskin." In the entire room, he missed exactly two first names. One was a Jim he called "John," and the other was just as close. I thought it was amazing that anybody could do that, and I was glad to learn that part of what the course did was to teach you how to remember names by associating them with something ridiculous. There was a guy named Trezie, and I remember thinking, *He looks like an oak tree with two big old eyes.* Buzz associated my name with "baskin' in the sun."

I did pretty well in the class. There was a prize for the best speech each week, and the night I told the story about giving the speech in Oklahoma City, I won. The prize was another book that came to mean a lot to me: *How to Win Friends and Influence People* by Dale Carnegie.

In fact, they liked me enough to ask me to come back and help with the next class. It was the way they groomed and then hired their instructors. I always wished I'd taken them up on it, knowing how much more I could have learned, but the time I spent in those classes was cutting into my production time, so I didn't.

Chapter 14

Working With
The Union

*I learned all I could about the company
so I could make myself more valuable.*

Avco was a union shop, but the local—
Local 735 of the International Association of
Machinists—seemed weak, and I didn't have any
interest in joining. In fact, only about thirty of the
one hundred or so guys in my department were
members. Then one of my fellow workers talked to
me about joining just as the union was negotiating
a new three-year contract.

"I'll tell you what," I told him. "If you get the
raise you're going after, I'll join."

About two weeks later they announced that we
had gotten the raise—I think it was seven cents an
hour—and so I joined. Once I did, I decided that if
the union was good enough for me, then everybody
ought to be in it. On breaks and at lunch I talked to
everyone in my department who wasn't a member,
and I signed every one of them up except for one
guy, and nobody could have gotten him to join.

The business agent for the union was so impressed that he decided I'd make a great committeeman, and he nominated me at the next meeting. Once I was on board, I studied the agreement between the union and the company and saw where Avco was getting around the seniority requirements for advancement with a system of ratings. An A rating qualified you for a better job, things that were a little more technical, that demanded a little more knowledge or leadership ability. The rating and those jobs always seemed to go to people the company liked rather than according to seniority, the way they were supposed to, and there were no tests or even formal job descriptions.

I talked to the business agent about it, and he said, "You need to go to people on the floor by seniority and get them to file grievances about the way they handle those A-rated jobs." I talked to each of the guys, from the most senior on down, and asked every one to file a grievance so we could bring this thing to a head and get it changed. Most of them didn't want any part of a grievance procedure, figuring that would get the company mad at them, until finally I got to Joe Hunt. He filed for an A rating and got it, and that convinced a few more to try, and they got theirs too.

From then on, I went after anything that didn't seem right. I was a little Napoleon out on the floor, getting into battle after battle and winning more often than not. I'd see that the company wasn't following the contract on something, and I'd go to the big honcho in the front office. Once I started, I never would back down.

I would approach the department foreman first, since most of the time he was involved in whatever was going on. I'd go to him, and he'd cut me off short. He and his supervisor, the department manager, never did want me to go to the front office, but finally I'd sign out on union time and head that way to talk to the head personnel man. Rather then let me go there, the foreman would back down and change what I wanted changed. He knew he was in the wrong, and eventually he'd figure out that it would be best to put the fire out in the department rather than let it get to the head honchos.

I finally got the department straightened out, although the company had a pretty negative view of me by then. Still, whether or not they thought I was a troublemaker, they knew I was a good worker. I'd been one all my life. I wanted to get ahead, and I knew I had to improve myself to do that. On the floor, I was always a leader, and the company took advantage of that. If they wanted to get an extra tail assembly or two produced, the foreman would talk to me, and I would talk to the guys and get them to work a little harder to help the company out.

My department attached big aluminum skins to the frame of the tail sections of those B-47s. Some of the rivets were three inches long. One man would hold a bar behind the aluminum sheet, and another would shoot rivets into it. It was exacting work because if you did it wrong, you could ruin a big, expensive piece of aluminum.

Ultimately I had my sights set on an office job, something that would give me the chance to quit working with my hands and start working with my brain. I really wanted to follow in my brother Art's footsteps. Then there was the fact that the noise involved in using rivet guns day in and day out wasn't doing my ears any favors—I lost the hearing in my left ear because of that job.

I learned all I could about the company so I could make myself more valuable, and I decided to take some courses. Now that I had a high school diploma, I signed up for night classes in engineering drawing at the Nashville campus of the University of Tennessee. I learned to read blueprints in another course. Finally I earned my own A rating, which I knew would qualify me for the kind of job I wanted.

The company didn't see it that way. I think they were a little scared of me because of how adamant I was about fighting for what was right on the factory floor. I stayed on the floor for two years with an A rating, but finally they couldn't look past how valuable I might be to them in a more responsible position. They decided they wanted me on their side. They talked to me about applying to become an assistant to the department foreman. I'd be keeping track of inventory and ordering parts for the department. In return, they wanted a gentlemen's agreement that I would lay off the union troublemaking, since I would be working with management. It was a good opportunity, and I agreed.

From the beginning, I liked it and did it well. I had a good memory—I got to the point where you could show me a part, and I could tell you what the part number was. I always seemed to be right on top of inventory and orders, and my bosses came to depend on me.

My desk and the foreman's butted up against each other in the office, and at first it was a little uncomfortable, given all the times we'd squared off over one thing or another. Finally one day I could feel him looking at me. He got up and walked around my desk. "You know," he said, "for a while

I was planning to come to you and tell you you'd better get off my back. In fact, I was going to fire your ass. But then I knew you'd take it to the front office and make a complaint. I knew there'd be a big rigmarole, and I decided against it."

We laughed about it, and eventually we put all those old squabbles behind us.

I had that job for two years and enjoyed every day of it. I liked the company, and I knew I could go places. Then, early in 1957, with business slowing, Avco announced a layoff. It would be done by seniority under rules set out in the contract, and they gave me a choice. I could take an eight-cent-an-hour cut—I was earning about seventy dollars a week—or I could hold my A rating and take a layoff, knowing I'd be called up by seniority for an A-rated job when things turned around.

I thought about it long and hard, and then I talked to the foreman.

"I've worked hard to get where I am," I said. "I went to school and have done everything I could to get ahead. If we've come to a place where I can't even hold my own, I think it's time for me to go look elsewhere."

"I'd really appreciate it if you'd stay," he said. "Take the pay cut. It'll come back around."

"Look," I said, "you can't help it and I can't help it, but I think I can do better." I took the layoff.

Just about that time, Ford opened a glass plant in Nashville. They were offering ten dollars a week more than I was earning at Avco, so I applied and got a job as an inspector. The plant made windshields, side glass, and back lights for several Ford cars and trucks. The glass was annealed, ground, and polished on-site, then we inspected it and shipped it out.

I didn't like the job much, but I was glad to be earning more. I was bringing home about eighty-nine dollars a week, which was good money. I bought the first decent car I ever owned that year. It was an Oldsmobile that had belonged to country singer Faron Young, who had traded it in on something else.

Theirs was a union shop, too, and I joined the United Auto Workers, although I never did get active with them. I worked at Ford for about a year before they announced the layoff that led to that fateful want ad.

PART II
SUCCESS

Chapter 15

Regional Manager

*The new job meant that I was going to
have to learn the two skills that would be
absolutely central to what I did
as a manager—hiring and motivating.*

For all the positive influence Jack had on me,
he apparently wasn't doing himself any favors. I
was never sure what soured his relationship with
the company, but something did. I'd been there
about a year and a half when Phil White, our
agency director, came to town and asked me to
meet him at our office. When I got there at 11:00
a.m., he was in a meeting that had started at nine.
Finally the door opened, and Jack walked out. He
just looked at me and didn't say a word. Phil took
me in and told me that the company had let Jack
go and that they wanted me to take his place as
regional manager. I hesitated, and he said, "We've
got confidence in you. We know you can do it."
I said yes. It would be fifteen years before I saw
Jack again.

I had been the company's number one agent my
first full year on the job, and I was new premium

leader in my second year. Now, in the fall of 1959, just eighteen months after joining the company, I was part of management.

That did have a downside. My office duties would keep me out of the field part of the time, which meant I wouldn't earn as much money selling. I'd collect a small percentage on the sales of each of the men who reported to me, but I was still going to take a good hit. It's one reason very few people really make the transition successfully. When you get into management, you have to bring on enough people that those small percentages add up to what you were earning with the big percentage you had on your own sales. Most guys flunk out, and at first, I lost a good amount of income. I had a talk with my boss, M. W. Newton, who was able to get me a little more salary, which helped while I made the transition, and I decided right away that I was going to spend as much time in the field as I could, management or not. Jack never went out and sold. I did. I always managed to spend at least the afternoon and most evenings in the field, so the dip I experienced at first didn't last long. I had never been afraid to work long hours, and that served me well here.

The new job meant that I was going to have to learn the two skills that would be absolutely central to what I did as a manager—hiring and motivating. We had a secretary who processed the applications, filed paperwork on sales, deposited checks, and handled our day-to-day dealings with the company, so I could concentrate on finding and inspiring good salesmen.

Recruiting became the biggest and most important part of my job, and I devoted several mornings a week to it. I was always on the lookout for agents. My basic recruiting tool was the same small, inexpensive newspaper ad Jack Schooley used. It said we were looking for an "order taker," listed potential earnings of $200 or $250 a week, and gave our phone number. That "order taker" wording was important because a lot of people were like me—they didn't think they could be salesmen. It helped to have that little inspirational talk with a prospect first, to get him fired up about the possibilities. I wanted to see if a man could get excited about a job that had unlimited potential— if he was willing to work hard enough. I wanted to know if he was the kind of man who could believe in himself and who could handle the idea of being his own boss.

The attrition rate for salespeople is really high. Most wouldn't stay all that long, and you had to hire ten or twelve to find a good one. I looked for desire. I wanted a go-getter, somebody itching to go out there and set records, but separating those who could do it from those who just talked it could be tricky. I won't ever forget hiring Melvin Brown. I hired another guy at the same time—a big talker I thought was going to be a supersalesman. He acted like he was going to set the woods on fire. On the other hand, I didn't think Melvin was going to do much of anything. Anybody would have thought the other guy would run circles around him.

It wasn't ninety days, though, before the other guy was gone, while Melvin turned into a great salesman, a good producer who stayed with me right up until he retired. Eventually I got pretty good at figuring out who had real potential, although there were always some I'd miss.

Motivating agents was something I'd seen Jack Schooley do every day, and I followed his lead. I didn't play Earl Nightingale's records, but I talked about motivation and desire, hard work and persistence. I worked to keep those guys focused, to get them to the place where they'd reach for their dreams, put themselves out, and go a little further than they thought they could. I wanted to jack up their competitive spirits, and having everybody announce sales goals for the week at the meeting helped.

Salesmen, especially insurance salesmen, are their own breed. They were mostly men. Now and then I'd get a good, solid female agent, but they were rare. I'm not sure why.

Most salesmen wash out, and I wanted to keep those who made the grade motivated. When you lay out the path of success for them and let your own passion for the business shine, they'll pick up on your enthusiasm and work harder. Pretty soon they're thinking, *You know, I just might be able to do this.* They'll put forth a little more effort, and when they see their names on that leader board, they'll work even harder to move a little higher.

I didn't have that many agents working for me that first year, but in 1960 we did enough business that I was named the company's Manager of the Year, beating managers in all thirty-nine states where we did business. It meant another banquet, another award—the President's Distinguished Award—and another speech.

That was also the year my mother died. She was just fifty-five. She had been heavy all her life, and she had diabetes, which she never took care of. I'd see her eat things I knew she shouldn't be eating, and she developed heart trouble, which is what killed her. It was too bad because she and my dad had really settled down in her later years.

His drinking slowed down a lot, and they didn't fight nearly as much or as hard as they once had. She died as my career was taking its first big steps forward, and for all the troubles she had and all the turmoil she could stir up, I knew I owed her a great deal.

Chapter 16

Learning To Close The Sale

Selling is about knowing when to talk and when to listen, and listening is much more important.

You don't have to be a big talker to be a salesman. In fact, despite what people think, people who've got big personalities and spend a lot of time talking can be the worst at it. Selling is about knowing when to talk and when to listen, and listening is much more important. That's when you learn what to say and when to say it. The best salespeople don't talk a lot, but when they do talk, people listen because there's meaning in what they say. Silence is generally more effective than talking once you've stated the facts and made your appeal. It's not that hard to overstate your case and talk yourself right out of a sale, and the "almost" sales, the ones you just can't quite close, all have one thing in common—they pay the same amount of commission. Nothing happens until a sale is made, and someone makes a sale at each and every presentation—you sell them or they sell you! A true professional learns to close the sale.

The biggest obstacles to overcome in the insurance business are affordability and bad experiences people have had with other insurance companies. When people thought they couldn't afford a policy, I had to make them see that they really couldn't afford to be without it. More than half the people I approached in those years didn't have insurance, and I had to sell them on the idea of insurance in the first place. I had to get past the idea that it was just an extra bill, something they hadn't been paying and didn't need. It helped to get them thinking about friends or relatives who'd experienced unexpected health problems.

"How many people in your own neighborhood have you seen faced with sickness and huge hospital bills?" I'd ask. "There are probably some in your own family who've been through that."

"Yes," they might say, "my cousin," and they'd tell me about his or her problems. Then it would be a matter of convincing them to act before they faced the same thing, and I'd often use the stories they had just told me to close them.

I tried never to let them give me a no, and I could always tell if one was coming. Before they could get it out, I'd say, "This is a plan that provides immediate protection. There's no waiting period. It goes into effect the day it's issued, so I can make it take effect today. You'd like that, wouldn't you?" That would often turn a no into a yes, and from there I'd just keep going.

"Let's go ahead and get this thing filled out and get you some coverage," I'd say. I didn't win every time, but I always did everything I could to postpone and then eliminate that no.

There were methods of keeping them in suspense about the details of the policy. I had the folder that outlined what was in it, but I'd leave it closed on my lap or on the coffee table and make them wonder what was in it while I talked. I'd get them to the point where they'd finally say, "Well, show me what you've got." At that point, the sale was made.

Three or four years in, I had four or five presentations down cold. They were canned, and I could draw on memory to do them in great detail. They were the product of years of knowing both how important this coverage could be to someone and how best to convince him of that. The last presentation I learned was aimed at the single hardest person to sell—the young man whose dad had given him a great start in life. Maybe he had given him a job in the family company or a nice big piece of property for his home. This was someone who felt like he could manage his money better than any insurance company could. I didn't run into guys like that very often; there'd be maybe three or four of them in a year, and they were obvious. They knew they were doing well, and they were cocky. It took a while, but finally I developed a presentation and a close that would work even on them.

"John," I would say, "you know, coming into this nice home it's very obvious—you can tell that you have worked hard, and you not only provide but you provide well for your family.

"John, you have a beautiful wife ...," and I'd look her right in the eye, or if she wasn't that pretty, I'd say, "You have a lovely wife ..." and look her in the eye "... and three fine children. I know in your mind there is nothing too good for this wife and this family. Is that right?" And he would agree.

"And you've worked hard, and the reason you

have worked hard is the love you have for this wife and these children. As time goes on you will continue to work hard to provide even better than you have today. Isn't that right?"

"Yes," he would say.

"But, John, wouldn't it be sad ... here you are working as hard as you can to keep everything and provide better than you have, if suddenly ..." and here I would slap my hands together or bring my hand down on the coffee table, "... something struck and you found yourself in a position that you couldn't even keep what you already have?"

I would let the silence build up for a moment.

"All I'm offering you"—and I would touch him as I said this—"for today, John, is to be able to guarantee that you can keep what you already have. That's all insurance is. And I know you want to keep what you already have, don't you?" A lot of times I would ask his wife the same question.

I'd be so focused on the person and on my presentation that I'd block out everything else. If I had a trainee out with me, I'd always make him sit across the room somewhere, out of the way, and I'd get so engrossed in the sale I'd forget all about him. Then when I finally closed and was taking the application, I'd look around, and there would be my trainee, still with me. I had one agent named Ed Wood who came out with me and thought I was the greatest salesman who ever walked. I remember one time he spoke at a sales meeting, and he described what it was like watching me work: "I watched him put on his white mittens and stroke them ever so gently, and then he'd get right up on the edge of his chair while he was making that pitch and he never leaned back in that chair again until the sale was made."

A hard sale—a real hard sale—might take an hour and fifteen minutes, sometimes an hour and a half. When I was that far into one, I used to say, "Sam, I appreciate you. You're a smart man. You're making me earn my living. You're asking questions, Sam, that have teeth in them. You want to know what you're buying. There's nothing wrong with that. Why do I like a prospect like you? Because, Sam, when you do buy this, you're not a wishy-washy buyer. You're going to have all your answers before you buy. You're not going to be someone who carries it for a while and then drops it and ends up needing it and not having it. The good thing, Sam, is you're going to have this when you wake up at three o'clock in the morning, and you tell the wife, 'Get an ambulance. I've never felt this way before. I'm sick.' You don't have to think about who's going to pay your bills. You'll have in your wallet a card that's going to admit you to that hospital. All you've got to think about is getting well. What's that worth to you? It's hard to put a price tag on it, isn't it? It's almost impossible."

And more often than not, I'd close him.

Chapter 17

Growing

There was no stopping us.

By the end of 1961, I had ten agents working for me. They were doing well and I was selling better than ever, and at the end of the year I won Manager of the Year again. We added a few more agents in 1962, and I won it that year too. The company gave me a vacation in Nassau, and Sadie and I left Nashville on January 16, 1963, for Miami, where we boarded the S.S. *Bahama Star* for our trip.

Among the people I hired in those early years was Winda Lingerfelt, who worked for me for many years and became a good friend. He was just nineteen when he first strolled into my office. He had a spark about him, but I could tell, as I told him all about the job and how much it was possible to earn, that he doubted everything I said. I was pretty cocky by that time, and I figured I could show him as easily as I could tell him.

"What are you doing this afternoon?" I said.

"I don't have any plans."

"Would you like to ride with me and I'll show you how this is done?"

"Yeah," he said. "Sure."

I took him to Franklin on two or three sales calls, and although I've heard him tell the story a million times through the years, it's always fun to listen to. He sat in that first living room with me, absolutely sure the people I was talking to were never going to buy.

Why don't we leave? he thought. Then he watched as I worked with the couple's interest and questions and turned them into a pitch that really perked them up. *Are these people really going to buy?* he thought, as I led them down the path and closed them. He was amazed at how easy it looked.

Winda came on board and was a really good salesman through the years. I seemed to be able to motivate him. Once I needed some extra sales production, and I called Winda and gave him a real good one-on-one motivational talk. Then I handed him a couple of leads in Fairview and said, "Go down there and show me what you can do." He went down and made five sales, turning in the biggest single day he'd ever had.

When he came in the next morning, I said, "Winda, I want to thank you for proving one more time that my system works. You don't know what that means to me." By the time I was done expressing my honest-to-goodness appreciation, he was all fired up again, and he went back down there and made more the second day than he did the first.

He was talking to the other agents, including Marion, about the pep talk I gave him and the boost in sales he got because of it. The next time I saw Marion, he said, "You know, I guess I need to go in there and let you talk to me too."

Winda has been my number one supporter

through the years. If anybody's ever been sold on me, it's him. Time and time again he has said, "I owe you. I give you credit for everything I earned through the years. I learned the principles of how to sell and how to do business from you." Still, there were a couple of times when the grass looked greener somewhere else, and he would go off and work for another company. In between, he'd come back and work for me.

"The only mistake I made," he said, "was not sticking with you all the way through."

Cecil Ryan came to work for me on April Fool's Day in 1962. I had known him most all of my life. He and Marion and I spent a lot of summer weekends together, cooking steaks and hamburgers in the backyard. He had seen how much money I was earning in the insurance business, and he asked if he could go with me on a couple of calls.

"Sure," I said, and one afternoon we went out to Donelson. I made a few calls and sold two policies. I earned something like $250, and on the way back to the office I said, "Here, take fifty dollars." He said, "No, I don't want any money," but I said, "It's worth that much to have you come out here with me." Not long after that, he was working for me. He was twenty-eight and he started as an agent, but I could see that he was talented enough that I wanted him on my management team. He and my brother Marion became my right and left hands through the years, training hundreds of people and overseeing sales regions for me. Cecil got to know most of the business inside and out, and when I started designing policies later on, he was somebody I'd consult because he had a lot of good ideas.

Finding guys like Winda and Cecil who could sell was one way to expand the business. In 1963, opening a branch office seemed like another good idea. We had some old furniture in the office on Nolensville Road, and I rented a trailer, put a couple desks in it, and took it all the way to Knoxville. I found somebody on the street to help me unload the desks and set up shop. I ran an ad in the local paper and hired a couple of people and moved one of my agents, Gordy Balch, in from Nashville to be manager.

I took over Bankers Service Life's office in Blytheville, Arkansas, too, and found they had a manager who just wasn't getting the job done. I terminated him and tried others but was never successful in finding someone who could run it. Finally I closed it. The Knoxville office lasted longer, and we had some success there, but never as much as I would have liked.

Back in Nashville, there was no stopping us. I was expanding on Jack's ideas, carrying his message of confidence and hard work forward. His advice was serving me well on a personal basis too. I was still motivated by his pep talks and by the books and records he'd introduced me to. Just as important, I remembered what he said about saving money. I never touched those premium checks—they went straight into a savings account. Two or three years in, the amount had grown from that first $75 check to $500, $600, and $700 a month. Then I began putting an extra $100 or so of my front money in with it. Soon that became $200, then $300 and $400, and before long I was setting aside $1,000 or $1,200 a month. I wanted that money to be safe, so every time an account got close to $20,000, which was the limit of what was federally insured at the time, I'd open another. Eventually I had ten or twelve accounts in different banks.

Once a year Sadie and I would take all our bankbooks and make the rounds, getting the interest posted. That would qualify us for a gift—a toaster, an umbrella, a waffle iron, or something else of value. We really enjoyed that day every year, picking out gifts and loading them in the backseat and trunk of our car. Given where we'd come from, it was a big thing for us.

We weren't much on extravagances, but we were living better almost from the start. In the early '60s, Sadie and I bought our first boat, a bright yellow sixteen-footer with a white deck and a fifty-horsepower outboard motor. We started spending nearly every weekend on Old Hickory Lake, often with Marion and Dot, and sometimes our friends Jimmy and Marian Thurman, and we all learned to water ski. We had wonderful times together, and it didn't seem extravagant at all to buy something that was such a part of our family's enjoyment and togetherness. All of us had kids, and it felt like one big extended family.

One weekend, Marion and Dot, Jimmy and Marian, and Sadie and I rented tents so we could spend the night on the lake. Despite the fact that I had been a Boy Scout, I'd never been on a camping trip, so I didn't know the first thing about setting one up. Neither did anyone else. We struggled with those things until a guy camping nearby saw us and came over and helped. Once we got them up, we had a great time, and pretty soon we all bought tents of our own.

That first boat was a good one, and we would take it to Center Hill Lake in Smithville, which was much deeper, with sky blue water surrounded by deep green woods. A few times we went to Dale Hollow Lake, which was even deeper—the water was so clear it looked like a tinted mirror. Ferro Fiberglass, where Sadie worked, had a lovely three-bedroom house that floated on the lake, and we were able to use it several times.

We enjoyed longer getaways too. We had been traveling to Florida for vacations since shortly after we were married. We bought a twenty-foot Shasta trailer in 1961, then a twenty-seven-foot Avco motor home in 1963 and a thirty-two-footer three years later. We took Sadie's parents to Florida once, and I'll never forget her dad's smile as we began passing orange groves. He asked at one point if we could stop so he could get out and pick one from a tree. I knew it was something you weren't supposed to do, but we stopped and let him pick one. We put it on the dashboard where we could see it, and it sat there in the sun through the whole trip until it finally dried out.

We used to travel for Shriner events too. I had joined the Masons not long after I got into insurance and had worked through the three degrees, entering the Shrine by working through both the Scottish and the York rites. Early on, I joined the motor corps. We met in a huge parking lot on Sunday mornings and practiced the maneuvers on our motorcycles, getting ready for meets. Just two weeks in, another rider and I ran into each other, and I fractured my arm, which Sadie didn't like at all. But I recovered, and she liked meeting new people as much as I did, so I kept at it. We had a lot of fun going to regional and national meets and attending Shrine conventions all over the country.

We worked hard and had tough inspections conducted by Marine officers. We stood at attention with our uniforms on, and each of us had to have uniforms and motorcycles that were spotless. If there was a bit of dirt anywhere, they'd find it.

My competitive spirit served me well in the motor corps. It wasn't long before I became lead rider, the one who calls and leads the maneuvers. We started winning championships right away, and over the years we won ten national titles with me on the lead motorcycle.

Those trips with the Shriners were just one more aspect of the great life Sadie and I were living. We always enjoyed dining and dancing, and we did all of it while living well within our means. We were definitely beginning to enjoy life in a way we never could before I got into the insurance business.

As our financial situation improved, Sadie kept her eyes peeled for a bigger house, and one night she talked about one she'd seen in South Nashville on Darlington Drive. I didn't want to take off work to look at it until Saturday because I always felt like I was losing money when I wasn't out selling, but finally she persuaded me to go the next day. I liked the house well enough that I signed the contract for it that morning and then went on to work. We moved in, and when the paperwork came and I saw the breakdown of how much interest I was paying, it made me sick at my stomach. I thought, *What in the world have I done?*

But the contract said you could pay as much as you wanted on the principal over and above the current month's payment, and I decided I would do that as much as I possibly could. I worked extra hard, and I paid two and three and sometimes four extra payments a month. I paid that house off in two years and still managed to keep putting those renewal checks into savings accounts. I realized that in no other profession except insurance do you start building down-the-road income with each sale. You earn money on the initial sale, and then, as long as people renew a policy you sold them, you earn money year after year. You can start building your retirement from your first day on the job.

Not long after we bought the house on Darlington, our family grew again. Sadie and I decided we wanted another child, and on September 5, 1963, almost fourteen years after we had Randy, we had a second son, Roger Scott Baskin.

Less than three months later, the nation went through the only event I've ever seen bring insurance sales nearly to a halt. I learned early and still believe that the insurance business is impervious to recession. People need insurance in good times and in bad, and nothing seems to affect that, including bad economies. A good salesman can do well no matter what. But on Friday, November 22, 1963, the assassination of President John F. Kennedy did to the insurance business what it did to the rest of the country. People were glued to their TV sets, in shock that something like this could happen. People got back to work the following Monday, but it was a good month or six weeks before people wanted to talk about buying insurance again. Nothing since—not even 9/11—had that kind of effect.

Chapter 18

A Greater Challenge

*Fourteen months after Union Bankers
bought out Bankers Service Life,
I was the leading regional manager
for the entire company.*

The house on Darlington quickly became a
family affair. Marion and Dot bought the house
behind us—their backyard butted up against
ours—and our friends Jimmy and Marian Thurman
lived just two doors down. We'd all get together
most weekends, grilling steaks, relaxing and
enjoying each other's company. I had a basketball
goal set up in the driveway, and I spent a lot of
time shooting foul shots. I got to where I could hit
about seven out of ten. Jimmy was the competitive
type, and he and I would bet each other on who
could hit the most. I'd always take his money.

We also spent a lot of weekends at one of the
lakes in the area, boating, grilling steaks, and
enjoying ourselves. Around this time, I bought
a nineteen-foot Sleekcraft inboard, and I soon
wished I hadn't. Very seldom did we go out and
come back under our own power. At some point

during the trip I'd be unable to start it, and we'd have to be pulled in. Every now and then I'd have somebody work on it, but they never did get the problem corrected. My experience with that boat made me a believer in something I'd always heard—the two happiest days for any boat owner are the day you buy one and the day you sell it. I know I was happy to get rid of that one.

Soon after we moved in, I won a trip to the World's Fair in New York from Bankers Service Life. As Sadie and I pulled out early one morning, we took Roger, who was just a toddler, to Marion and Dot's house. I handed him to them, then just stood there looking at him and crying. He was so small, and it was the first time we were going to be away from him.

"Go on," Marion said. "We'll take good care of this boy." It took me quite a while to peel myself away and walk out to the car. We had a great time, but it taught me a lot about just how much I loved our boys.

By that time, Sadie and I were well settled into a wonderful married relationship. We had married as teenagers, with no real experience of the world, and we had to stumble our way into life and marriage. My temper had made things tough on us now and then in the early years, and it took a big episode to help change that.

We would be going along fine—two young people in love, with a baby and jobs and big dreams—and then every six months or so my temper would flare over something and we'd have a big fight. As often as not I'd get into the car, slam the door, and speed off. Sadie would follow me out to the car, and sometimes she'd grab the door handle, trying to get in. It's a wonder she didn't get hurt.

Once, when Randy was seven or eight, Marion and Cecil and their wives were at the house on Ennis Road, and we guys wanted to go off and do something or other. The girls wanted to go and we didn't want them to and it turned into a big argument. Sadie said something smart to Marion or Cecil, and it made me mad. She and I got into it, and I threw one of my fits and stormed to the car, with Sadie not far behind me. I tore out of the driveway, throwing gravel as I went. I looked in the mirror just in time to see Sadie falling on her face and Randy frantically jumping up and down beside her. I went back and ran over to her. There was gravel in her mouth, and she wasn't responding.

I picked her up, and I sent Randy for a cold rag. I put Sadie in the car, and she and I and Randy took off toward the Goodall Clinic in Smyrna. Sadie still looked unconscious. I had the window down and the air vent on her and I talked to her as I was driving.

We got to the clinic, and the doctor examined her and asked what had happened. We came to the conclusion that she was doing her best to get my attention and that she had gone too far and lost control and just sort of went into a faint. The best I could tell, she had come around pretty quickly and was playing a part a little, but she definitely had my attention, which was what she wanted.

She and I knew we had to do something. We went home to bed and lay in each other's arms. We talked about how much we loved each other and how silly and uncalled for it was for us to fight that way and for me to act the way I did. We were still talking when the sun came up.

We gave each other a promise that night that we would never again do anything to hurt each other, and we pretty well have lived by that promise all these years. I can't say we don't have a few little spats here and there, but there were never any big problems after that. That conversation is probably the best thing we ever did for our marriage, which was good to start with, but has been truly great since then.

There was a big change in my business life, too, around that time, and it was nowhere near as positive—at least, it didn't seem so at first. I had been with Bankers Service Life for five years when, out of the blue, Union Bankers of Dallas, a much larger company and one of our competitors, bought us. I hated the thought of working for someone I'd gone head-to-head with the day before.

Several things conspired to make the road tougher for a while. Regional offices were structured differently with Union Bankers; I would essentially be an independent owner/operator rather than a part of the company, as I had been with Bankers Service Life. I had received a salary as regional manager in addition to the commissions I earned on sales and overwrites. Bankers Service Life paid the rent, utilities, and other expenses. At Union Bankers, those things would come out of our slice of the pie. Because of that, I quickly closed the Knoxville office.

My percentages went way up—I received 60 percent of the first year's premium on everything I sold rather than 30 percent, as I had for Bankers Service Life, and a 15 or 20 percent overwrite rather than 5 percent. The Union Bankers contract was vested, which meant I would draw my commission for renewals even if the contract was terminated. That hadn't been the case with Bankers Service Life. With Union Bankers I would no longer receive a salary, and at least at first I took a financial hit.

When our first monthly production report came from Union Bankers, I was in tenth place among regional managers. I was used to being number one, and I was very disappointed. I looked at the top of that list at the man who'd finished first— his name was Jack Gardner and he was regional manager for the company in Mississippi—and I couldn't believe the figure I saw. I was earning more than anyone I knew, and according to this, he was earning four times what I was. I took a copy of the statement home that night and showed it to Sadie.

"You know that guy didn't earn that kind of money," I said. "I can't imagine why this company would falsify something like that."

I was sincere. It was beyond my comprehension. I couldn't think big enough to imagine myself earning that kind of money. As I looked at that list, I could see myself beating the guy who was number nine, and that's the goal I set. The next month I beat him, and so I set my goal higher, and a month later I jumped the next man, and the next month I jumped two. A little less than a year in, I saw my income rise to a level where I knew Jack Gardner was reachable. I pulled out the sales sheet and looked at his numbers and then at mine. *They weren't lying to me*, I thought.

Finally, fourteen months after Union Bankers bought out Bankers Service Life, I was on top, the leading regional manager for the entire company. I held that position for the next sixteen years.

The recognition and rewards for sales achievement were much bigger with Union Bankers than they'd ever been with Bankers Service Life, reflecting the much bigger size of the company.

In fact, the incentives and bonuses could get pretty extravagant. In 1965, our office did well enough that I and eight of my best agents and our spouses were given a trip to Europe. Marion and Dot, Cecil and Joanne Ryan, Eugene and Jean Wright, Gordy and Lena Balch, John and Martha Ratcliff, Dewey and Charlcie Burden, Bob and Ann Whitson, and Winda and Sue Ann Lingerfelt got on a plane for a three-week, eight-country tour. We enjoyed ourselves immensely, but when we got back, my secretary, Betty Watwood, told me that the minute we left, the agent I left in charge had begun stealing business. He recruited every agent I had in the Nashville office and used my leads to sell for the competition. It looked like he'd been plotting it ever since he heard we were leaving and had been able to work out a higher percentage for himself from the other company. Betty figured it out pretty quickly and stopped giving him leads, but by then he was off and running.

The thing that was surprising is that he'd been with me two or three different times over a period of several years. I hadn't expected anything like what he did. I fired him right away, but most of my sales force was gone and we'd lost three weeks of production. To top it all off, I found out that while we were gone my son Randy, who had just started driving, had taken Marion's car without telling him and rolled it over. It was an extremely expensive free trip.

There was nothing to do but roll up my sleeves and get back to work. Fortunately, all my best producers had gone with me. We started building leads and selling again. I was determined to make up the lost ground, and we did. We set yet another sales record that year.

A year after all that happened, the agent came crawling back.

"No," I told him, "you've blown your chance with me. I left you in charge! I was across the ocean, and you betrayed me. You stole every man I had and used my leads to sell for somebody else. That's about as low as it can get. Even with that, we came back and set a new record this year. I've learned I can do it without you. I don't ever intend to work with you again."

It really hurt him because we'd had a good relationship, but the whole episode drove home to me the fact that ultimately all business is dog-eat-dog.

Chapter 19

Continental Insurance Service, Inc.

"Boy, do I feel good!"

By the mid-sixties, I saw the need to carry life and health policies other than those offered by Union Bankers. We were running across more and more people who didn't meet the criteria for our regular coverage but could qualify for "substandard" coverage, which involved higher risk and higher premiums. I didn't really want to go after that kind of business, but it was hard to avoid. Say we talked to a couple and the wife was in good health, but the husband had a heart condition.

"I can give you coverage," I'd say. "Your wife will qualify for a standard policy, but your condition means I have to offer you another kind of policy. It's got a higher premium and lower benefits, and you'll have to wait a year before it covers anything related to your heart."

We ran into that sort of thing all the time, which

meant that unless we offered those policies, we were losing a tremendous amount of business. So, in August of 1965, I formed Continental Insurance Service (CIS) as an umbrella under which I could do business with other companies. All it took was a business license and agreements with the companies I wanted to represent.

With CIS I had my own salesmen offering a lot more products. Union Bankers didn't like the fact that I was selling their competition's policies, but I was a self-employed contractor, so they didn't have a say in the matter. Plus, I was bringing them so much business they weren't going to complain as long as I didn't take a product that competed directly with one of theirs.

I had ten or twelve products with Union Bankers, including an accident policy and a good basic hospitalization plan with three benefit levels, each with its own premium rate. I carried a good cancer policy from Atlantic American out of Atlanta and some basic hospitalization policies and eventually a Medicare supplement from Iowa State Travelers out of Des Moines. Union Bankers and Atlantic American both had low-cost cancer policies—Atlantic American's was better—that might bring in $60 or $80 or $100 a year—"gas money" policies, I called them—and we rounded out our offerings with some substandard policies.

Building an agency, I relied more than ever on the things Jack had taught me. One of them was that success has a look. A regional manager should dress better than the average person. He should drive a nice car and live in a nice house. He should be the person everyone looks up to, the guy everyone wants to be like. He should act the part of a successful person. A manager in the field, on the other hand, needs to tone it down. He should also drive a nice late-model car, one that's dependable and looks good without being flashy. Agents in the field resent it if someone else in the field shows them up too much—it's just human nature. Of course, everyone needs to dress sharp, to let customers know you care about appearances and about detail. If your appearance is sloppy, you can't blame people for wondering if you're sloppy with your follow-up or your work habits in general.

It's pretty universal that you get 80 percent of your production from 20 percent of your sales force. Your job as manager is to keep bringing them on, training them, and letting the cream rise. Most aren't going to be great at it, but when you find one who is, you've really got something worth nurturing. I was always looking for that go-getter, and those are rare. Actually I always liked the term go-giver, as in someone who gives service.

Weekday mornings were about finding guys like that. The weekly meeting was about keeping them motivated. After the first couple of years, I moved the meetings from Saturday to Friday—everybody needs family time—but the purpose was the same. I had to keep those good agents pumped up. I'd open and close every meeting by having everyone in the room holler as loud as they could, "Boy, do I feel good!" something I got from the Dale Carnegie course.

I wanted everybody setting goals—big goals. At the first of the year I'd have every salesman take out a piece of paper and write his sales goal for the year, just like Jack had done. They wrote, "A winner never quits and a quitter never wins," on that sheet and kept it in their pocket with their change. At every sales meeting, you had to reach into your pocket and pull out that note. If you couldn't, it cost you one dollar. If you were a manager, it cost you five dollars.

In those meetings, I wanted to recognize the doers—the people who were really selling. I wanted to pump them up, to instill a sense of pride in them and raise a sense of competition in the other salesmen. I'd call their names one at a time, and each guy would say how much he'd written that week. We'd all give him a hand, and I'd write the number on a production board at the front of the room.

We really talked up the numbers. You had to let those guys know you expected a lot out of them. If you didn't expect them to produce, they wouldn't, and I always expected them to do something big. Everybody wanted to put big numbers up to get the attention and accolades that went with them. Nobody wanted to admit to having a bad week. I always gave a lot of credit to anybody new who had really produced. I wanted them to feel great, to be proud of a job well done. That helped give them self-confidence and the desire to do it again. Sometimes when you're out in the field, just picturing the praise you'll get in that next sales meeting can lift you up when you need a boost.

Then we'd get to that week's sales leader. We had a big, comfortable "big dog" chair sitting up front, a takeoff on the phrase, "If you can't run with the big dogs, stay on the porch."

"Well, let's see," I'd say. "Who's gonna be sitting in the big dog chair this morning? Winda Lingerfelt, come up here! Tell us how you did that!"

We'd give him a big hand as he walked up to the front of the room. He'd say a few words about selling, and then he'd sit down in that nice big chair for the rest of the meeting.

Once that was done, I'd give them a pep talk. I might discuss motivation, confidence, or overcoming negativity. I used a lot of things I learned from Nightingale and Napoleon Hill in those meetings, just like I did in my life. Then I'd have somebody with a big mouth close the meeting.

"Come on, let's raise the roof!" he'd yell, and everybody'd join in as he shouted, "Boy, do I feel good!" I wanted people to hear us down the block.

"Boy, do I feel good!" wasn't just a line with me. I did feel good. I was extremely confident in my abilities—*cocky* might be the right word. I'd been Manager of the Year three times. My sales figures and those of the office as a whole were the best in the country—the best in the company's history—and they were only going to get better. During that period, I finally got out of selling in the field altogether. With my agents' production and my overwrite checks growing every year, I was more valuable in the office, hiring, managing, and motivating agents and managers, dealing with other agencies I could bring on board to sell our products, and looking for new markets. Those were the years when I became a marketer, the role I considered perhaps my most important for the remainder of my career. The future was as bright as it could be.

It was bright on a personal level as well. I was earning more than I ever had and saving more money than I ever dreamed possible. All those lessons I'd learned from Jack kept paying off.

My first priority with personal spending was to make sure my family was well provided for, and I was proud of our house on Darlington Drive. But then one day I got into a conversation with the marketing director for Union Bankers as he visited Nashville.

"Randall," he said, "that house of yours is nice enough for most anyone, but don't you think you need one that's as different from those up and down the street as you are from the average insurance executive? You need one that has the Randall Baskin look, one that makes a successful statement."

He got me thinking, and Sadie and I started spending our weekends looking at homes. Two that we saw really interested us. One was a large one-story house that had a gorgeous façade, with columns and nice brickwork, and a cedar shake roof with an arch topped by a copper dome, with a big window on either side trimmed in copper to match the dome. The other, a smaller two-story home, had a den with a cathedral ceiling that I really liked too.

We hired an architect to draw up plans combining the best of both. Then we found a lot we really liked at 836 Old Hickory Blvd. in Brentwood. It was owned by Patterson Construction Company, which had already laid the foundation for a demonstration home on the property. We bought the property and had them add to the foundation so that we could use it with the plans our architect had drawn up.

I knew that paying cash was the way to go, and every month I would go to the contractor's office with my checkbook. The secretary would write checks paying all the bills, and I was able to write off the sales tax. I don't remember the amount of savings it came to, but it was sure worth doing. Paying cash usually lets you get the things you want for less money.

As construction progressed, I always did my best to get home before dark so Sadie, Randy, Roger, and I could inspect what had been done. Sometimes, when I was late, we did our walk-through by flashlight. This was going to be our dream home, and we were really excited about it. On the days when they got a lot done, we were happy. On the days they didn't, we were disappointed. On weekends we would spend hours out there, walking through and around the house, planning what we would do in this room or in the yard, deciding things like where we wanted the pool.

One Sunday afternoon after church as we were making our inspection, a neighbor drove up. He looked at the house and said, "Boy, I would hate to see the monthly payment on this one."

I laughed and said, "You just have to learn to sign your name." I didn't want to tell him I was paying cash. He probably wouldn't have believed me and would have thought I was just putting on a big-shot act.

It took a year, but finally it was ready. We named our new home Pleasant Villa, putting the name on a mailbox we had placed in stone. We received many compliments, and in fact I sold copies of the plans to two people who wanted to build homes just like it, one in East Nashville and one in East Tennessee. We were as proud of that place as any family has ever been of a home.

We shared a lot of memories in that house on Old Hickory. When we moved in, Randy was just entering his teenage years, and Roger did a lot of his growing up there. There were a lot of differences in their personalities and in the way they were raised. You want your first child to be perfect—healthy, happy, and well behaved. Fortunately, that red medicine had cured whatever it was that made Randy such a sickly child. From there on, Sadie and I did our best to teach him right from wrong. We'd slap his little hand when he grabbed something breakable or got out of line in some way. Eventually, though, we realized we weren't going to raise a perfect child, and we eased up on the discipline. We had worried because of the struggles he had with his schoolwork, but he'd gotten a little better through the years, settling in to B's and C's.

Roger was a much healthier baby than Randy. I'd see him, fat and happy in his crib, and think back on those long nights with Randy, hollow-eyed and crying. I was really glad it was easier for Roger and for us.

We were in a lot better financial shape when Roger was a baby, and I'll admit we spoiled him. It started with his eating. He was healthy and a good eater, which Randy never was, and I think Sadie wanted to make sure he stayed that way. She'd spoon feed him, holding that little jar of baby food, just shoveling it in as fast as he'd gobble it up. I used to get on her about feeding him so much so fast, but she'd always say, "If I stop, he'll quit eating." Roger was a big eater from then on, turning into a chubby little boy.

Randy was old enough to be helping in the business by this time. He'd round up a couple of his friends and go out with Marion and me, putting flyers on car windshields to help drum up business. He'd help put sales packets together, stuffing brochures and applications into the folders the salesmen carried. I really wanted him to follow me into the business. It had treated me so well, giving me more than anything ever had. I wanted him to have that kind of opportunity and know that kind of prosperity.

I also saw to it that he got some outside work experience. He took a job nights and weekends behind the counter at Brooks Pharmacy, a place owned by a friend of ours at the corner of Trousdale and Harding Place.

He was also old enough to have a mind of his own. As he became a teenager, he showed his first signs of getting into trouble. Those are the years when it's going to happen if it does. We didn't know it at the time, but he was crawling out his bedroom window to go visit his girlfriend. At one point I got a call from a teacher at Overton High School telling us he and a few other boys had skipped school. Then he and some friends broke some windows out of the school building with rocks. I made him take the money he was earning with his drugstore job and pay to have them replaced.

In July of 1967, Sadie and I took Roger with us to Washington, D.C., for a Shrine convention. While we were gone, Randy decided he would take his friends and the boat to Center Hill Lake. We got a call that he had hit something and sunk the boat. Fortunately, no one was hurt, but the engine went under and had to be rebuilt completely. Randy also wrecked Sadie's new car once not long after he'd gotten his license.

Then there was the time I got a phone call one night after he'd been in another car wreck. He'd stolen some gasoline out of another car and was running away when he hit a telephone pole. I was upset—disgusted, really. I couldn't for the life of me understand why he would act up that way. He had the money to buy the gasoline. I worked and he worked. He was doing it just for the kicks. I think that was the incident that started to wake both of us up and made us realize we needed to confront reality. This was serious. When you take someone's property, you can wind up in jail.

Fortunately, Randy was good about learning

his lessons. He was a pretty typical boy, testing the boundaries, trying to stretch his wings, and he came around after he'd gotten caught at something he shouldn't have been doing. I'm convinced that his love for his mother and me helped turn it around following another episode.

When he was about seventeen, he came into the house one night and asked me to come out on the patio.

"I want to talk to you," he said.

He confessed that he'd been stopped for speeding. The police officer came up to the window and took his license, looked at it, and asked if he was kin to me. Randy said he was, and the cop said, "I know your dad. He's a good man. He's done a lot of good for a lot of people."

Randy was crying as he told me. He said, "The policeman told me, 'If it wasn't for your dad, I'd haul your ass in.'"

He told me nice things other people had told him about me too. He'd cry a while, then talk some more. It was obvious he was really touched by the things people had said.

"Dad," he said, "I love you and I just want you to know how proud I am to call you my father."

I have treasured that memory for a lifetime, and Randy went on to become a good young man. He became a better student through the years and decided to attend Middle Tennessee State University in Murfreesboro, not far from where I'd grown up and about forty miles from where we lived. It surprised me a little just how much it affected me to take him to the campus. We walked into his dorm room, which was as plain and barren a room as I'd ever seen. It was dingy looking, with just a bunk bed, not even curtains. All of a sudden

I felt unbelievably sad that he was going to have to stay in a place like that.

I guess it struck me, too, that when you drop your child off at college, you know he's leaving and that he's never going to come back home the way he was before. From that point on, he would come home as a visitor.

I knew and he knew that he was coming into the business. He'd been doing one thing or another for the company pretty steadily since before he was a teenager. But that didn't make the thought of the profound change in our relationship any easier. Sadie took that day pretty well, but I cried pretty much all the way home.

Chapter 20

Going For
The Big Time

*With that endorsement,
the business really turned a corner—
and I lost most of my fear of speaking!*

If we were going to keep expanding the way I wanted, I knew I had to be more aggressive about hiring agents. Bringing them on one at a time just wasn't efficient. I wanted to bring on whole agencies with sales forces overseen by guys like me. I'd send someone down to the state insurance department to spend a couple of days going through records and getting names and contact information for all the agencies and agents in our market area, especially those who sold policies similar to ours. We'd go first to the manager or owner. If we could recruit him, we'd have access to all his agents. If we couldn't, we'd let him know we were going to go after them individually. We always had a lot of top-notch products we knew those guys would want to sell, so we had a real advantage. The managers would figure that out, and eventually they'd take contracts with us in self-defense. In a dog-eat-dog world, I knew how to eat dogs too.

As our sales force grew, it became more important to hire good managers. You had to look for men who could motivate people, who could keep the fire alive inside them. You wanted someone who could inspire an agent to do what was best for the customers because that would be best for him too. You get back what you put out—I believe that. If you give hatred, you receive hatred. If you give love, you receive love. When a man sells insurance, he's got to feel in his heart that he's doing a great job for his customer. He's got to do it to the best of his ability in the right way.

We were always looking for better ways to get the word out, and one was sitting right in front of me. *The Tennessee Magazine* reached seventy-five thousand customers of the Tennessee Electric Cooperative Association, made up of the rural electric cooperatives that helped bring electricity to rural areas—like the one I grew up in. Plenty of people outside the cities got the magazine, and they were exactly the people we were trying to reach going door-to-door. We took out an ad and gave contact information, and it became a great source of leads from the late sixties right through the eighties.

Another great way was to look for groups to endorse our company and its policies. That would open the door to their membership and give us lots of potential customers.

At one point I had my eye on the Veterans of Foreign Wars. Most of its members were World War II veterans who made up a great pool of potential customers for our group health and accident policy through Union Bankers. I met with the VFW's Tennessee commander, Jim Cowan, several times, showing him what we had and telling him what a good fit I thought it was for his members. He liked what he saw but said it would have to be voted on. The state convention was coming up in Memphis. Would I be interested in presenting the idea to the three hundred delegates there?

I knew I was good in a sales meeting, but I still wasn't all that comfortable talking in a formal setting before hundreds of people. I contacted our home office, and they said they'd send M. A. Chandler, the director of marketing. Then it turned out he couldn't come. Instead, he sent the company's executive secretary. Two days before the program, my boss, M. W. Newton, who had come down to Memphis, talked to me.

"Randall, if you get this endorsement, it could earn a lot of money for you and for the company, couldn't it?"

"Yeah, it could, Newt."

"You've worked hard getting on this program," he said. "You've done a lot of legwork preparing to enter this market. You could present it a lot more effectively than anyone. If you want this deal, you'd better get your ass on that stage and talk to them yourself."

I knew he was telling me right. I had to dig down deep and get over my fear of speaking, which I knew was all in my mind, once and for all. I had taken the Dale Carnegie course, and I had to go back to those principles. I just needed to express my honest and sincere appreciation, then make sure my topic was something that everyone had in common. I could look at it as a door-to-door sales call with a big crowd of people. I phoned the company on Friday afternoon and said, "I've made up my mind. I'll do it."

I called up every bit of confidence I had gained from Dale Carnegie, and at ten o'clock Saturday morning, I walked out to that podium.

"I want to thank the commander," I said, "and I want to thank all of you for giving me the opportunity to show you something that's really going to be exciting for you. Right now, my associates are handing out a pamphlet. It outlines a group-type health plan we're offering for you here today, something that would give your members great coverage at a great price. I'd like to go through it with you, and then you decide whether you want to make it available to your members."

By that time, I was fired up. I had hit just the right note from the start, and I went through the policy, point by point, telling them just how good a deal it was and why it made sense for them to buy it and recommend it to their friends back home. I walked off that stage three feet off the ground. I knew I had that endorsement. I could feel it.

M. W. grabbed me as I came off and poked me with his elbow. "You did it, boy!" he said. The delegates voted yes right after I left, and we had a huge new market. We began running an ad on the back cover of the VFW's state newspaper, touting the benefits available to members. Gordy Balch started sending a guy to VFW posts to talk up the policy and line up prospects, and then Gordy would go in and close them.

With that endorsement, the business really turned a corner—and I lost most of my fear of speaking!

Chapter 21

Managing—Stacking My Blocks

*"If you're going to be a salesman,
be a top-notch salesman."*

There are all kinds of things to watch out for when it comes to salesmen, but the two most likely to screw him up are liquor and women. The first great agent I hired really sold a lot of insurance for a couple of years, but then he met a woman and divorced his wife. Within a year, his production was half what it had been. That was still good for an ordinary salesman, but it was bad for him.

Then there was one of my district managers. He was a great salesman, a guy who just knew how to sell insurance, but twice a year or so, he would go on a drunk. He'd get started and run for a week or ten days, then sober up and go back to work. I paired him once with a guy I'd just hired. I had no idea he was an alcoholic, too—you never do until they start drinking. I sent them to Memphis on a selling trip, and they stayed in the same motel room. Well, they both started drinking and got into an argument that turned into a knock-down, drag-out fight. I found out when the motel manager called me and said the room was in shambles and there was blood everywhere. He sent me photographs of the room and told me he wanted me to pay for the damage. I think it cost me six hundred dollars to cover the repair bill. I never did see the new guy again, so I took the six hundred dollars out of the district manager's commissions.

To be a successful manager, you had to be a financial advisor, a marriage counselor, and somewhat of a preacher. I had a good salesman in Lebanon, Tennessee, who had gotten into serious financial problems, and he and his wife were about to break up. They fought like cats and dogs, and now and then I'd get a call at two o'clock in the morning to bail him out of jail. I'd get him out and sit with them and try to get them on the right path. I knew this guy had it in him to be a great salesman and just needed guidance. He was worth trying to save. Finally I called Paul Durham, the preacher at Radnor Baptist Church, which Sadie and I attended, and asked for his help. I took this couple to his house and had him counsel them. He met with them several times, and they were able to save their marriage.

I remember guys who came to work for me living in apartments or tiny houses, driving beat-up cars and wearing shabby suits, and in a few years they'd be in nice homes with two or three automobiles and a bass boat, wearing good-looking new suits and taking great vacations now and then. I always loved it when they did well like that, and I was always pleased when they showed their appreciation for the guidance I'd given them.

One of the guys who really warmed my heart was Will Mattox, who came to work for us in East Tennessee in the early 1970s. He drove a little old car to his first awards banquet, and he wasn't dressed very well. He was under Cecil Ryan's management team, and Cecil did a great job training him. The second time he came he had a nice-looking suit on. The third time, he won a big prize, and before long he and his family moved into a nice home. By the late seventies, he earned Man of the Year honors in applications. I used to talk to him and guide him, and he was always appreciative for the chance to follow the system I laid out.

"Randall," he would say, "I'm so happy to be a part of the Continental team." He was enthusiastic about being a leader and about his own success, and I was always really proud of him.

Overall, you have to work with them, knowing that what happens is mostly out of your control; they're going to do what they're going to do. But when you really help someone when he's down and out and stick with him, and then he finally comes around, it's a great feeling. There was a guy in Missouri named Mike Tomlin who hit a rough patch in his life and gave up selling insurance. Most of the companies he dealt with canceled him, but I stuck with him. I loaned him money when nobody else would, and finally I got him to close a couple of bars he'd opened and get back in the insurance business. The effort I put into helping Mike in those days really paid big dividends. He became my number one supporter and producer through the years, and he was always a big help when I created new insurance products. To this day, he is still one of my very best friends.

Keeping the productive agents or those who had potential was as important as hiring and motivating them, and I don't think you can do either unless you can read people. It's a skill you learn if you're going to become a good salesman, and it becomes more important when you're an executive. I can read a guy's face. I can tell when he's with me and when he's not. I can tell who's eating out of my hand in a meeting and who isn't. I remember once speaking to a roomful of agents, and I had everybody in my pocket except for one guy. He'd been with us for a few years, and he was always on fire in these meetings. He listened to me. He believed in me. This time, he was looking out the window.

"We're fixing to lose him," I said to my brother afterward.

"How do you know?"

"I was watching," I said. "He's on his way out."

Sure enough, the following week the guy quit.

I never could teach my managers how you did that. It's an instinct, a gut feeling. It's about the way they shift in their seats or don't look you in the eye. You don't know how you know. You just know.

Dealing with a guy who's become discouraged or who's thinking of giving up on himself or the business can be tough, but if you know a guy's got potential, it's worth it. I remember a situation in 1968 with an agent named Roger Birdsong. He'd been with me for three years, and he apparently decided he'd had enough of selling. He was with a crew working the Pulaski area when he decided he was ready to give it up. He was going to send his sales kit and paperwork back to me with one of the guys in the crew. I got wind of it and called him.

"Roger," I said, "who gave you that kit?"

"You did."

"Don't you think you owe it to me to bring it back and personally give it to me?"

"Why do you want me to do that?" he said.

"Well, you know we've been fair to you and always treated you right," I said. "I just feel like I gave it to you, and you need to give it back to me."

"Well, if you want me to, I will."

He started driving back to the office, but then he got to thinking it was silly to have to come back and see me. He was quitting, and he might as well just quit and go on. He started to turn around, but then our conversation got to him and he headed my way again. He almost backed out two or three times, but finally he walked into my office and gave the paperwork back to me.

"Okay, you're quitting," I said. "Now what are you going to do?"

He had some fuzzy plans that didn't really amount to much. I asked him some questions, honestly looking to find out where his head was, what he wanted out of life, and how he planned to get it. He knew that I was successful at what I did, and he knew that he hadn't gotten anywhere near his potential. Sometimes when a guy is in that position, he can't see past the surface of successful people. He doesn't see what's gone into it, all the sweat and self-motivation. He sure isn't thinking about the times when the guy across from him failed and picked himself up again.

So I told him about not being able to go into that house in Lebanon, thinking they'd never buy. I told him about going through a whole week and getting to three o'clock on Friday with just thirty dollars in sales. I could see him loosen up a little, and he told me about some of the tough days he'd had. I told him another story or two. After we'd talked for thirty minutes, I pulled out a set of justice scales I brought out on occasions just like this. I set the scales up and picked up a big wooden block with SUCCESS written on it.

"Roger," I said, "from where you're sitting, success looks big and heavy. It looks that way because you're looking at the guy who's already successful. You're looking at the guy who already owns the big house on the hill. But have you ever wondered how that guy got started?"

I set the block on one of the scales, and he watched as it sank to the tabletop. The scale on the other side hung in the air, empty.

"Stop and think a minute," I said. "What is success? It's a lot of things, but I like Earl Nightingale's definition: 'Success is doing a predetermined thing that you decide to do deliberately, and doing a good job of it.' If you're going to run a service station, run the finest one on the turnpike. If you're going to be a teacher, be a great teacher, the one that students will talk about for the rest of their lives. And if you're going to be a salesman, be a top-notch salesman. Learn to grow and develop in your company.

"How do you get there? How do successful people get started? Well, you know that for every action, there's an equal and opposite reaction. You become what you think about. In the insurance business, or in any business, for that matter, it all starts with desire. Not just any desire—a burning desire, as if your life depended on it."

I picked up one of nine smaller blocks sitting on the table. It said, DESIRE. I set it on the empty scale.

"You cannot wish for a number of things that

are equally important. You must decide on the one thing you want the most and create a desire to have it. Set that as your goal and go after it."

I set the block marked GOAL beside DESIRE.

"Setting your goal is the most important thing you will ever do. You must know where you are going. Once you do, your natural ability will assist you in achieving it. In this case, it might be earning a certain amount of money. You want to aim at something that will comfortably support your family. You decide how much money you would like to earn in a year's time. Then break that down into monthly, weekly, and daily por-tions. That gives you your goal. You'll have to write so much insurance in order to meet that goal. That might mean you have to write three policies a week, or five, or seven, or ten. You decide that. You look at that figure every Monday morning as you go out to sell. That's when you apply your de-termination."

I set the block marked DETERMINATION by the first two.

I kept going, through blocks marked PERSISTENCE, SELF-DISCIPLINE, ENTHUSIASM, FAITH, and POSITIVE MENTAL ATTITUDE. One by one, I talked about them, about the importance of each element. The final block said, DO IT NOW, and when I placed it with the other eight, the scales were finally in balance. SUCCESS had risen to its rightful place.

"You know, Roger," I said, "when you apply these principles, success is automatic. You couldn't stop it if you tried. Be enthusiastic. Be excited about what you're doing. Be determined. Work hard. Success will be there. It's going to come. You're going to reach your goal. Picture it in your mind. See yourself already achieving it."

Roger took his kit back, drove down, and caught up with his team in Waynesboro. He earned more money that week than he had ever earned with me in a month, and he told the guys on the crew, "If you want to be successful, you just need to go and let Mr. Baskin talk to you."

He was a much better salesman after that.

I'd use that balance and those blocks five or six times a year on some guy who was down and out, someone I knew had it in him to do better. I'd go through the whole thing with him, make him see what I'd been through, let him know that success was inevitable, but that you had to give yourself to it completely. You had to put everything you had into your dream. That talk would find that spark inside him, and when he left, he'd have a streak of fire shooting out of his butt. There's something about seeing that balance, about watching the cumulative weight of those attributes, that set of commitments, lift that big block that says SUCCESS, that stays with a guy.

Chapter 22

Back To The Field

*"Apparently, you've forgotten how to
sell insurance," I told them.
"I'm gonna come down and teach you."*

Even the best of companies will experience a
slump now and then. In the big scheme of things,
ours were never all that bad, since we were always
at or near the top in national production, but I
didn't like them. I would do whatever I could to
get the guys stirred up and excited again. In fact,
the last time I went out in the field, it was for that
purpose—to build a fire under my salesmen.

It was in the early '70s, and I was still regional
manager for Union Bankers. It had been five
years since I'd been out selling door-to-door, but
production was down and I had a crew in Paris,
Tennessee, that had been there for two weeks and
hadn't sold much of anything. Monday morning as
they left, I told them I'd be there Wednesday.

"Apparently you've forgotten how to sell
insurance," I told them. "I'm gonna come down
and teach you."

I went to the office Wednesday morning, finished
up the work on my desk, and went home to pack

my clothes. I was really depressed at how bad we'd been doing. My stomach was twisted in knots, and I went into the bathroom. I picked up *Think and Grow Rich* and sat on the john reading the chapter on faith. I always read that chapter when I needed a lift, and I needed one then. I sat there so long, absorbed in that book, that by the time I got up the circulation in my legs had been cut off. But Napoleon Hill had done what he always did—I was on my way to thinking positive.

The drive to Paris took two and a half hours, and I used the time to think over what I'd read. I checked into the motel at five o'clock.

I'm going to sit and read this chapter again, I thought, and when they come in, I'm going to have a fired-up meeting and then I'm going to take somebody out there tomorrow and teach him how to sell insurance.

But then it hit me: *It's been five years since you've been out there, Randall Baskin. Do you know how to sell door-to-door anymore? If you're going to teach them by tomorrow, you'd better get yourself out there tonight and sharpen your claws.*

I went through my briefcase and got my brochures in order so I could put my hands on everything I needed. Then I found a blank lead card and wrote down "Sarah Johnson. Paris, Tennessee."

I drove away from the motel, and at the first house I visited I made an appointment for Friday. Then I stopped at another and asked the lady if she knew where Sarah Johnson lived. I heard the back door slam as her husband came in. She called to him and said, "Do you know Sarah Johnson?"

"Well," he said, "you might go down to where the road goes off to the right. There are some

Johnsons back in there." The three of us got to talking, and I made a sale.

It was just before sunset when I drove back to the motel, on fire from the success I'd had. One of my salesmen was sitting there in the lobby reading a newspaper. I said, "Man, you must have had a great day, since you're sitting here in the golden hours reading the paper."

He looked a little sheepish, and I said, "Let's go. I'm gonna teach you how to knock on doors after dark."

He thought I was joking.

"Come on," I said, and I led him out to the car. As we drove off, I said, "I'm going to knock on the door. If I motion to you, grab your briefcase and come in."

At the third house I knocked at, this old guy drew me a map with a lot of detail in it to show me where Sarah Johnson lived. We talked as he drew, and I found out that he was a member of the VFW. I showed him the endorsement we had.

"This is your lucky day," I told him.

"It's my bedtime," he said.

"I ain't gonna take but a minute."

"You better not because I'm going to go to bed in a minute."

I signaled to my salesman, who brought his briefcase. I went quickly over the program and sold the guy right there. I was hot as a firecracker.

We went back to the motel, met the other salesmen, and went out to this little restaurant. When the waitress came over, all the guys started cutting up with her.

"It's obvious they've been here quite a few times in the last couple of weeks aggravating you," I said.

"Yeah," she said.

I pulled out my card. "I'm Randall Baskin. If I ask you a question, will you be completely honest with me?"

"Yeah, I will," she said.

"Now, these guys have been eating here for two weeks. Have any of them taken the time to explain to you how you might qualify for a group-type health insurance program? I want you to be honest with me."

She looked at them and then at me.

"No, I'm afraid not," she said.

"Well," I said, "I'm not going to be that way. I think more of you than that."

I turned the card over and said, "Write your name and phone number there."

She did, and I said, "What are you going to be doing in the morning?"

"I've got to help my aunt at eight thirty."

"Well, how about if I come see you at eight?"

I went to her place the next morning and made the sale, and when I came back to the motel, the rest of them were still shaving and getting dressed. I showed them what I'd done, gave them a pep talk, and sent them back out into the field. Whether I'd inspired them, shamed them, or both, they did a lot better from that point on.

Chapter 23

Faith And Charity

*"Radnor Baptist Church
got me started on another kind of giving
that has given me more good
experiences and memories than most
anything I've ever been a part of."*

Every day as I drove to and from the office I passed Radnor Baptist Church, our family's spiritual home. Our faith was an organizing force in our lives, the thing that made the talk of material success meaningful as a symbol of a life lived with purpose. Paul Durham, the pastor, had become a good friend.

I'd think now and then about the way faith and career intersected, and there came a time when the thought made me uncomfortable. Back before I got into the insurance business, I was dropping fifteen dollars a week in the collection basket. That was a lot of money when I was earning seventy-five or eighty dollars a week, but once I got in the insurance business and was earning a lot more, I was still giving fifteen dollars. I had a lot of really good days in the field, and there was only so long I could pass that church and think about my paychecks before my conscience got to bothering me.

I need to up my ante, I thought. So, one morning in 1970 or so after a really good day, I got to the office and wrote a check for one thousand dollars—today it would be like writing one for ten thousand dollars—put it in an envelope, and mailed it to the church. It felt good, and I never really missed the money. Then, before long, after another really good day, I did it again. And then again. I did that seven times, and while I was at it, I got my weekly offering up to where I thought it should be. I've tried to be good to the church I attend ever since.

Around that time, Radnor Baptist got me started on another kind of giving that has given me more good experiences and memories than most anything I've ever been a part of. One fall, the church came up with a list of families who really needed help. Those of us who wanted to do something for them drew a name and bought Christmas gifts for that family. Delivering those gifts, seeing the appreciation in the eyes of those parents and kids, felt so good that Marion and I began doing it every year.

I knew exactly what it was like to be the people in those families. That's who we were during the Depression, when people gave us clothes and we shopped for subsidized food. Now we had the chance to give people new clothes, good food, and toys, games and other things I never would have dreamed of as a boy.

Soon we were buying for five or six families. We'd get a group of women at church to help us with the shopping. We'd give them the sizes and they'd buy the clothes and shoes and pick out anything else they thought they'd like. Marion and I would stop early Christmas Eve at the Kroger store at Elysian Fields in Nashville and buy a ham and a turkey and all the trimmings for each family. The manager caught on to what we were doing and began giving us things. After a few years, he was giving us almost as much as we'd bought.

After we finished shopping, Marion and I would load up our cars with food and all those wrapped presents and go out and give them to the families on our list. Eventually we had to start using a truck to make our deliveries. Our own Christmas really couldn't compare to the joy we had in giving out those gifts, and I don't know that any Christmas since has ever been quite as good. We did it for twenty-five years, and it's one of the best sets of memories I have.

My success was also allowing me to spend more time with both my sons. Randy graduated from MTSU with a degree in business in 1971 and came to work for me. I was glad my father was still alive to see that and to see Randy get married.

Since I wasn't in the field anymore, I was home more and was a bigger part of Roger's day-to-day childhood than I'd been with Randy's. We were still spoiling them. I helped Randy with pretty much every big purchase he ever made, and Roger had everything he wanted and then some. You don't ever want your kids to have to go through what you did, in our case the worst of the Depression. It was that way for a lot of people our age. We knew what it was to have nothing and we wanted our kids to have everything we could give them. I'd see the families we were helping through the church and be reminded of my own childhood. I never wanted my kids to know that kind of hardship. Somewhere in the back of your mind, you know you're spoiling them, but that doesn't stop you. You forget sometimes that hard times make for tough people. Tough times help you appreciate what you do have. So many of the people I admired, the people who went from nothing to success, who wrote the books that inspired me, had been through hard times just like I had. In the words of the old proverb, we had no one to give us fish. We had to learn to fish on our own. Sometimes when the next generation finds that it comes easy, they lose respect for the connection between hard work and success.

Roger did better in school than Randy did, and that was one area where we didn't help him as much. Part of that, I think, is that Roger went to a private school, which took more interest and did a better job with its students than the public schools Randy had gone to.

Marion and Dot's son Mike was about Roger's age, and the two of them played together all the time. They were close like Marion and I had always been, and I was glad to see it. When we traveled, we took Mike with us most of the time, whether or not Marion and Dot went, although Mike was a lot more like Randy—more likely to roughhouse it, to play football and go swimming at the beach. Roger was more of an inside kid, and he never cared for a lot of that stuff. He was more reserved, and he never got into the kind of trouble that Randy sometimes found.

He was still on the chubby side, liking both indoor activities and sweets. I remember a family trip in our motor coach to Gatlinburg. Roger and I were sitting there one day, and he had this chocolate teddy bear. He pulled it out and looked at it.

"I'm gonna eat you and get you off my mind," he said, and he went ahead and ate it.

When he was young, he also had a temper—of course, he came by that honestly—but one episode taught him a huge lesson.

He took piano lessons every Thursday, and we bought a piano for him to practice on. There was a light that sat over the music stand and it would droop down over it and he'd have to push it back up into position. After a couple of times, he got mad and swung at it and hit it. Well, he caught his wrist just right on the metal shade and sliced a pretty good gash into it. The metal went right through a vein and he bled like a stuck hog. We took him to our family doctor, who got the bleeding stopped but said, "Roger, I can't do anything for you. You've cut the tendon too. You're going to have to have surgery, or you're going to lose the use of that hand." He sent us to Vanderbilt Hospital, where they sewed the ligaments together. They saved the use of his hand, but Roger was in a cast for six months. He must have thought long and hard about it because that slowed down his temper for good.

Chapter 24

The Spotlight

*"A living is made from 8 to 5,
but success comes after 5,
when the rest of the world is coasting."*

My desire for the kind of success that allowed me to be generous never wavered. I was motivated by the same things that motivated my best salesmen—a feeling of accomplishment, satisfaction at a job well done. Union Bankers had a monthly magazine, just as Bankers Service Life had, and nobody liked to see his picture in there more than I did. I wanted my agency to be the best in the company when it came to sales, and we were, pretty much every month, every quarter, every year. Between 1966 and 1968, CIS doubled its sales force and tripled its production.

I carried every issue of that magazine to my dad, who was living with his sister Maggie out near the town of Triune. Few people knew like he did just where I'd come from. He'd brag to everybody about what I was doing, and I was so glad he was alive to see it.

Dad lived to be almost ninety, and he died just

as my career was turning another corner, in 1972. That was the year I bought my own building, just a mile or so up the road from where our offices had been. Moving from 2720 Nolensville Road to 3709 Nolensville Road was another big milestone on my journey to success.

Not long afterward, I established my own weekly newsletter to do for our region what *The Blue Eagle* newsletter did for Union Bankers as a whole. I always felt you couldn't run a successful agency without one. Recognition is a great motivator. People like to see their names in print. You list your leaders to give them something to feel good about and give the other guys something to shoot for. I knew how much I liked getting awards and hearing Jack Schooley's secretary say he was always talking about me to new prospects, and I wanted everybody to have the chance to feel that way. I talked about my agents in meetings, gave them engraved plaques and vases, and rewarded them with everything from savings bonds to all-expenses-paid vacations to places like Hawaii, things they would treasure and remember for a long, long time.

The most impressive and longest-lasting recognition is in writing, and that's why I started *The Spotlight*. In the beginning, we printed copies on an old mimeograph machine that left ink all over the hands of whoever ran off copies. I'd list all the weekly, monthly, and yearly leaders for sales and applications, and feature the top salesman on the cover, which had a graphic of a man shining a big spotlight on a wall.

Inside, I'd announce new policies we were handling, talk about contests we were running, and update the salesmen on anything else that was important. We were always running contests—our Christmas contest was big every year—looking for ways to keep the guys excited and to keep them setting goals. We always had a slogan going—"Success for Me in '73" was one of the early ones. Every year we did a "March for MacArthur" competition in honor of John MacArthur, who owned Bankers Life and Casualty, which bought Union Bankers in 1974, and whose birthday was in March. He believed if you set huge goals in March, you'd break records and set the tone for the rest of the year. It was an approach I could get behind, and it always worked well for us. In honor of my birthday, we made one week a "March for Baskin" contest and urged everyone to push especially hard for sales. We tried constantly to break our monthly and yearly records, and more often than not, we did. We were almost always the biggest-selling region in the Union Bankers company. I'd also include something inspirational—slogans, pep talks, an excerpt from one of the motivational books, a cartoon that dealt with hard work or motivation—in the newsletter to help keep everybody fired up. I was always looking through books and magazines for positive quotes and sayings, and whenever I'd see something that fit the bill, I'd cut it out. Once I was in Chattanooga on business, and there was a country restaurant with walls covered with inspirational sayings and stories. I don't know how much time I spent there copying them down for the newsletter. I also turned again and again to Earl Nightingale and Napoleon Hill for quotes.

The Spotlight might have a piece called "The ABC's of a Good Sales Talk" with each letter standing for a specific tip, or it might have a ten-point program for success. It could talk about teamwork or decision making, the opportunities presented by problems, or keys to dispelling fear and worry.

In one issue, I listed tried-and-true statements a salesman could use to help close a sale. They were hard-nosed, realistic, and effective:

> "If you're having a hard time now getting by on your salary, how could your family possibly get along without it?"

> "You are a money-making machine and machines wear out."

> "Do you know of any other plan that permits you to will your family thousands of dollars before you have earned them?"

> "How much will be left from your present insurance after the hospital, the doctor, and the undertaker have been paid? Will there be enough to pay your widow's bus fare to work every morning?"

> "If you're not here to pay your boy's college bills, who would you rather have pay those bills—my company or your son?"

There might be a short item that ended, "The tragedy and the real waste lie in what we could do and could become but do not. Next time you say, 'I'm wasting time,' change that to say, 'I'm wasting myself.'"

I remember a saying that summed up my attitude about evening work when I was in the field, and I ran it in one issue: "A living is made from 8 to 5, but success comes after 5, when the rest of the world is coasting."

I also remember longer items that summed up my beliefs about the components of success. One I especially liked was by William Arthur Ward. It appeared in the September 9, 1974, issue:

THE WISDOM OF LOSING YOURSELF

If you are wise, you will forget yourself into greatness.

Forget your rights, but remember your responsibilities.

Forget your inconveniences, but remember your blessings

Forget your own accomplishments, but remember your debts to others.

Forget your privileges, but remember your obligations.

Follow the examples of Florence Nightingale, of Albert Schweitzer, of Abraham Lincoln, of Tom Dooley, and forget yourself into greatness.

If you are wise, you will empty yourself into adventure.

Remember the words of General Douglas MacArthur: "There is no security on this earth. There is only opportunity."

Empty your days of the search for security; fill them with a passion for service.

Empty your hours of the ambition for recognition; fill them with the aspiration for achievement.

Empty your moments of the need for entertainment; fill them with the quest for creativity.

If you are wise, you will lose yourself into immortality.

Lose your cynicism. Lose your doubts. Lose your fears. Lose your anxiety. Lose your unbelief.

Remember these truths: A person must soon forget himself to be long remembered.

He must empty himself in order to discover a fuller self. He must lose himself to find himself.

Forget yourself into greatness. Empty yourself into adventure. Lose yourself into immortality.

Firing up the salesmen might take the form of friendly competition with another agency that we'd write up in The Spotlight. I knew a lot of general agents with big agencies across the company. I'd meet them at Union Bankers conventions and keep in touch with them through the year. Jack Mollish was a great guy and a Union Bankers regional manager in West Virginia. We used to have contests with him and his agents. We'd talk them up in both of our newsletters and try to outdo each other. One year he beat us, and he sent me a drawing of a grave. "Here's Randall Baskin," he wrote on it. "Cause of death—beat to death by the Jack Mollish team."

I played up the rivalry big that year, and we came back and beat him and his district. I sent the grave drawing back with a note that said, "He has risen."

I put *The Spotlight* together for a long time. Now and then I looked for somebody to take over as editor, but nobody could ever do it to suit me, to get the punch in there I knew it needed, so I just kept writing it. I knew enough to mail those newsletters to the agents' homes so their wives could see them and feel involved. They like to see their husbands doing well, and I wanted them to see the numbers and the accolades.

The recognition I gave out in the newsletter and in the weekly meetings was all aimed ultimately at our annual banquet. That's where the weekly competition, one salesman going up against all the others for that little edge, came to a head. Every agent wants to see himself walking up there to pick up those big trophies and plaques amid all the applause and congratulations. Everybody wants signs of success he can hang on the wall in his office or place on the mantel at home. On top of that, I might give out watches, TVs, or diamonds, status symbols that added even more luster to success. It was all designed to keep everybody excited and to celebrate the achievements that seemed to grow bigger and better every year.

That competitive spirit was still a big part of my relationship with the Shriners as well. The motor corps, with me on lead motorcycle, had won ten national titles in a row. We were practicing twice a week—early on Sunday morning and on Wednesday night. After the Wednesday practice, we'd all go out to dinner. But finally I decided to step aside and let someone else take over. I liked being able to retire undefeated.

Then the corps was beaten in the very next Southeastern competition they entered, and they asked me to come back. Somehow, I let them talk me into it. We went back through another season of victories and made it to the national championship. We were leading and in the middle of maneuvers that involved circles within circles, a demanding and impressive maneuver, when all of a sudden I heard an engine racing. I looked around, and one of our guys had gone down. Of course, when that happens, you've lost the tournament. It was the first competitive race I ever lost. This time, when I hung it up, it was for good.

I threw myself into Shrine fund-raising as well. Shriners are well known for their children's hospitals and for the millions of dollars they raise to support them. For many years, we held a paper sale to raise money for the hospitals, collecting nickels, dimes, and quarters in cardboard holders. The year I became co-chair for our region, I changed the system. I was used to organizing, setting goals, and getting things done, and I thought through how we might do better for such a good cause.

We'd been asking businesses for a dollar or maybe five dollars, and I decided we should ask for a hundred dollars and give each business a nice plaque that had a picture of a Shriner carrying a disabled child. It was a chance for the business to get some real recognition with a classy-looking plaque for its generosity. Each year we'd ask them to send us a check, and we'd mail out a new sticker for the plaque. When I took over, $225,000 was the best year we'd ever had in our part of Tennessee. During the seven or eight years I was head of the drive, we raised that amount to more than $600,000.

Chapter 25

Florida

*I wanted to beat them
at their own game.*

My drive for achievement and success never wavered, but the way I channeled it evolved as my knowledge of the business world grew. A dozen years in, I knew that the real money in insurance lay in having exclusive rights to a product. Then every time somebody sold it, you'd earn a commission. I had never designed a policy, but I wanted to give it a try.

I saw that Standard Life and Accident did a great job with Medicare supplements, which came about in reaction to the 1965 introduction of Medicare, and I wanted to compete with them. I had no desire to sell their policies because they had too many agents. I'd be entering a field that was already crowded. I wanted to beat them at their own game. I started playing with their policy, tweaking and adding features to make it better. Then I went to Nashville-based Midwest National and asked if they would take it on. They agreed, and I took the next giant step in my career—I had my own policy in the marketplace.

Just as I'd hoped, I was able to compete head-to-head with Standard in Tennessee. When I introduced the policy in Florida, though, it didn't go anywhere. Orange State had an even better version, and we couldn't make headway against them. I started tweaking theirs to make it better yet and took it back to Midwest. They approved it, but then at the last minute the company president thought he'd better run it by the chairman. The chairman was an actuary, and he rewrote one small section, setting a limit on the benefits outlined in one part of the policy. It didn't hurt the overall policy, as far as I was concerned, but it meant we had to refile with the state insurance agencies. That pushed our rollout back another ninety days or so. When I did start marketing it, though, agents and customers loved it. I wrote the dickens out of that policy.

Then, after two or three years and maybe three million dollars in premiums, Midwest started getting nervous. If you're afraid of claims, you'd better not fool with Medicare supplement policies because it's a claims business. After a couple of years, the claims were coming in, and Midwest was nervous about the payouts coming down the road. Soon they'd had all they wanted, and they quit selling it.

Fortunately, I learned a lot in the process of designing and selling that policy, and the information served me very well down the road.

I was still feeding my desire for success with inspirational books, and one that I discovered around this time was one of the best. It's called *The Richest Man in Babylon*, and it's a collection of parables set in ancient Babylon. They were written during the 1920s by George Samuel Clason and later assembled into a book that dispenses basic, vital lessons in financial wisdom.

The book resonated very deeply with me. I had a taped version, and I listened to it a lot. It talked about living on less than you earn, which Sadie and I were very good at doing. It also said that one dime out of every dollar that passes through your hands ought to be put to work for you in the form of savings or investment as a way to build toward long-range goals. Those goals could be a big house, a better car, a condo at the beach, or money in the bank.

The man in the book talks about the fact that thinking you'd save a year's salary in ten years was only half right because the money, put to work for you, would actually produce another year's earnings. In ten years you would have saved two years' earnings.

I put the master copy of that tape along with a lot of records and other valuables in a lock box in a concreted safe I had installed in the building I'd just built. One morning I came in to work and found that someone had broken in and had beaten in the door of the safe with a sledgehammer. Those papers were scattered all over the floor, but there was nothing missing. They'd apparently been looking for cash and coins and didn't find any. There actually was money there—one thousand dollars tucked into an envelope—but they hadn't seen it.

As my older son Randy helped me clean up the mess, he saw and picked up the tape. Like a lot of young people, especially those who are doing well, he never saved much. He was a little reckless and hadn't buckled down financially. In fact, I was never successful in getting either of my kids to look at money the way I did.

But he had listened to the tape, and as he handed it to me, he said, "If I'd done what this tape said the first time I listened to it, I'd be a lot better off now."

I had done that and a whole lot more. I was actually saving probably seventy cents out of every dollar at the time. I had no bills except for utilities and insurance, groceries, and things like that. I was able to take vacations I wanted, and I'd helped Randy buy a couple of houses and helped my younger son Roger buy a condo.

"Randy," I said, "you've heard me talk about the three M's of success—Man at Work, Men at Work, Money at Work. The Man is you. You start out working hard. Then you start thinking about teaching a few people to help you, and you encourage them to work hard. Set things up where you can draw an overwrite, that ongoing percentage, on the people you train. That's the second—Men at Work. To apply the third, Money at Work, you must learn to save. The best way to save is to pay yourself first, as the tape says. For every dollar that you earn, you should save ten percent and put it to work for you." I talked about earning two years' salary rather than just one in ten years and said, "Once you get started, it becomes fun. The great thing about it is that it's a sure step that leads to success. It's a system that's worth applying, starting today. The trick is to do it."

Not long after that, Jack Schooley, who had taught me most of what I knew about life and business and whom I hadn't seen in fifteen years, walked back into my life. He came into my office out of the blue one day, and he and I went into the kitchen and had a cup of coffee.

He said, "Son, I've been around quite a bit since I last saw you, and just about everywhere I go, I hear your name. I'm proud of you. You've done a good job. And I'm proud I had just a little something to do with it."

I thanked him for all the things he'd taught me and for getting me off to such a good start in the business. I asked him what I could do for him. He said he wanted to keep his license active and maybe sell a little insurance now and then.

"I'd like to represent you," he said. I didn't have to think about it. I knew he deserved it for all he had done for me. I knew he was more boss than salesman, but I was happy to give him a contract. He sold maybe three or four policies, and I saw him just once more, when he stopped by the office to pick something up. A couple of years went by, and one day while I was out of town on a trip, I got word that he'd died. I didn't even get to attend his funeral.

But he was still part of the foundation of my success, which just kept coming. New business premiums topped $500,000 a year by 1975, and early in 1976 we expanded into Florida, Kentucky, Alabama, and Mississippi. By 1978, our production reached the $1 million mark, and the numbers on every weekly, quarterly, and annual report drove home to me the fact that dreams were attainable, that there was no limit to what someone who had desire, a plan, motivation, and the willingness to work hard could accomplish. Jack had also introduced me to the books that encouraged me as a dreamer, and during those years, somewhere in the back of my mind, the first spark of yet another dream flared up—the thought that someday, somehow, I might run my own insurance company.

If I did, it would have a lot of family involved. Roger had been just as involved in the business as Randy had been, starting the same way, putting together sales packets and putting flyers on windshields before he was a teenager. There was no reason to think he wouldn't join the company after college too. I took him to MTSU, just as I had Randy. I'm not sure it was quite as tough as it had been the first time, but I still cried on the way home.

It turned out Roger didn't like his bare dorm room any better than I did, but he dealt with it by making plans to live somewhere else. Not long after he got there, he sent me a newspaper clipping about a guy who bought a condo for his kids to use while they were in college. When they graduated, he sold it at a profit. Roger said he had a condo all picked out four blocks from campus. I just laughed. I had no intention of indulging his little dream. But he had pretty good powers of persuasion, and one Saturday I found myself there looking at the condo he'd picked out. He got Sadie on his side and told me all the details he'd thought through and worked out, and I bought it. Roger and two of his friends took it. That would give him two people to help him pay me rent.

At least that's the way it was supposed to work. As I've said, I had a knack for spoiling him. I never did see any of the rent money for the condo. He used some of what they paid him to fix the place up—through the years he'd developed a real eye for decorating, which he enjoyed practicing in the houses we owned—and the rest I guess he used as spending money. When it was all over, I did sell it at a profit.

As the money rolled in, I was always aware of my responsibility to the poor, to charitable organizations, and to the church that meant so much to me and Sadie. Radnor Baptist was a little church where I knew I could make a big difference, and in the late 1970s, when Pastor Paul Durham talked about the need for an auditorium, it just seemed natural for me to help out. I became the head of the bond committee that oversaw fund-raising. The auditorium cost a little over $600,000, and we put my name on the bond. Through the years, in addition to my regular contributions to the church, I made payments now and then toward that bond. As I signed each one, I would think, *I'm not personally liable for this debt, but I sure would hate for this church not to be able to pick up one of these payments when it's due, especially since my name is on it.*

And I felt good every time I did it.

Chapter 26

A Convention
And A
$250,000-a-year
Loss

People have asked me through the years
what really launched me into the big time.
I always say, "Losing a quarter
of a million dollars a year."

I always enjoyed Union Bankers conventions.
They were a chance to catch up with people I
didn't see the rest of the year and celebrate how
well the company was doing. They were great on a
personal level too. When you produce, they treat
you like a king, especially at conventions, and
we were producing like crazy. By the end of the
1970s, I had seventy-two agents, and we were
selling a lot of policies for Union Bankers, along
with everything else we sold. I had been General
Agent of the Year most of the years I'd been with

the company, and CIS won the Leading Agency Award in 1980.

The conventions seemed to get a little more extravagant every year. There were elegant restaurants and fine cars. They gave us the best rooms in great hotels, and you could order anything you wanted from room service. Given where Sadie and I had come from, it was almost unbelievable. A lot of guys would take advantage of the room service privilege, but she and I never did.

In 1981, the convention was held at one of the world's most luxurious hotels, the Hotel del Coronado in San Diego. I knew I'd be getting the royal treatment, but I had no idea how big it would be. The car that pulled up in front of the hotel for Sadie and me was a Rolls-Royce, and when we got to the banquet hall, we stepped onto a red carpet, Sadie in her long dress and me in my tuxedo. Kids ran up to us, holding out sheets of paper, yelling, "Mr. Baskin! Mr. Baskin! Can I have your autograph?" We were led up a set of steps to a backstage area and then out onto the stage through fog-machine haze before a huge hall full of elegantly dressed agents and their wives. Above us, on a huge screen, they were showing our entrance—cameras had been following us since we'd driven up in the car.

"Here he comes now," said the announcer, who was none other than Union Bankers president John Coffman, "the Man of the Year—Randall Baskin and his lovely wife, Sadie!" John and director of marketing Don Rutherford greeted us on stage as everyone stood and applauded. Sadie and I were just dumbfounded. I had won a lot of awards through the years, but no presentation had ever come close to this one for pomp. John was the greatest promoter I'd ever met, and he could make you feel like a king. He sure did that night.

They announced the big awards, and I won three of them. Each included a full set of elegant silverware. *What will we do with all that silver?* I thought. All these years later, we've still got it, and it's still a tangible reminder of a great career moment.

That was the last time I was on the receiving end of that kind of presentation by Union Bankers. I was still selling a lot of their insurance, but by then they were a smaller percentage of CIS's overall business. I was branching out, moving in other directions. I didn't know it yet, but I was on the threshold of another big career leap, and the spark would come two years later, at the 1983 Union Bankers convention in Dallas.

It happened after a speech by an agent from Texas who was doing a lot of business. There was nothing that stood out about him, and I don't remember what he talked about, but afterward I went up and introduced myself. As we chatted, I asked whom he was writing most of his business with. He told me a lot came from a little stipulated premium company—a smaller company with fewer requirements for reserve capital—licensed in Texas.

"They've got a Medicare supplement policy with a real neat feature," he said, and he told me how it worked. Most companies with Medicare supplements lost their shirts because doctors would run up their bills on them. The companies invariably pulled the policies off the market. This policy, the man said, would pick up costs Medicare didn't, but would never pay more in total than Medicare did. I thought it was brilliant. The policy had a built-in safety valve. *A*

bigger company ought to put that policy out there,
I thought.

I recognized it as a great idea, but I just filed it
away. I was already doing fine. Then, six months
after that conference, the second piece of the
puzzle fell into place when a friend called and
said one of the companies I represented, Iowa
State Travelers, was going bankrupt. At first, I
thought he was joking. I had been selling Iowa
State's hospital and Medicare supplement policies
for years, and their renewal checks amounted to
$250,000 a year in income for Continental. I was
blind-sided—I thought they were rock solid. I did
some checking, and it turned out another division
in the company had gotten in trouble and taken
them down with it, but the bottom line was the
same—I never got another dime from them.

We had fifty-six pending applications with
them—our agents had sold the policies, we had
taken out our company and agents' commissions,
which totaled 60 percent, and sent the paperwork
to Iowa State, which hadn't yet issued them.
That meant people had paid us for policies that
weren't going to go into effect. Some had been in
the pipeline for weeks and were calling, wanting to
know where their policies were and what we were
doing with their money. They had begun writing
the insurance commissioner's office, complaining.
The assistant commissioner was an old friend of
mine, and I called him.

"Be careful," he said. "You're not liable here.
Check with your attorney before you do anything."

He knew there could be lawsuits involving Iowa
State, and he didn't want to see me get caught
in the middle. My attorney didn't want me to get
involved either.

"This isn't your fight," he said. But I knew we were involved. People had given their money to us, not Iowa State. They kept calling. We put them off, saying we were working to get it sorted out. Those were probably the darkest days of my career. The unthinkable had become a reality. People thought we'd stolen their money. The spotless reputation we'd built up over the years was at stake. I wanted to make it right, but I couldn't risk the legal complications my lawyer and the commissioner were warning me about. I couldn't sleep. I felt helpless.

Our agents were in a tough position, too, since they had actually sold the policies, and it was in thinking about them that it finally came to me: I didn't do it. The agents did it. But maybe I could give them the money and let them make it right. They could replace the policies those customers bought with something similar— United American Insurance Company, for one, had a comparable policy.

It wouldn't be cheap—we were already losing $250,000 a year, and replacing the policies would cost me another $26,000 out of pocket—but it would be the right thing to do.

I was so grateful for the reading I had done through the years. I drew inspiration from the stories of so many people who had faced dark, troubled times and who had held on, digging deep to keep going and to do the right thing.

I went to my lawyer and told him what I had in mind. United American had agreed to write the policies. We could call the money I was advancing to the agents a loan, although I'd never enforce payment. That would keep us as a company out of the middle of things—we wouldn't be liable.

"Well, you might have something there," he said, "but I want our errors and omissions insurer to sign off on it."

I agreed. "Errors and omissions" provides what amounts to malpractice insurance, in this case making sure the new policy was equivalent to the old. That was an added layer of protection in case we missed something. It took them a couple of weeks to get back to me, and when they did, I told the man what was happening and what I wanted to do. He looked at me like I was crazy.

"Mr. Baskin," he said, "you don't have to do this."

"I know I don't have to do it," I said, "but I want to. This is my reputation."

"I admire your courage," he said, "because you didn't cause this problem, but I'll stand behind you."

He sent me a letter that gave me the go-ahead. I could tell our customers the whole truth: "We've taken a contract with an A+-rated company that has a very similar policy, and we're going to make your insurance good. It's not something we're obligated to do, but you paid us your money and we're going to see that you get a policy. It will take a little time, but we'll be there for you."

It took ninety days to get it sorted out and the calls kept coming in the whole time, but finally the agents came in, I wrote the checks, and we got replacement policies in effect.

I've always been grateful I bowed my back and did the right thing then. It kept our reputation intact. It also did something much bigger. People have asked me through the years what really launched me into the big time. I always say, "Losing a quarter of a million dollars a year." They look at me like I'm kidding, but I say, "I'm dead serious. It's the best thing that ever happened to me." That's because at that point I was ready to get to work on the idea I'd picked up at that conference—designing a financially sound Medicare supplement policy. And that was my entry into the big leagues.

PART III
THE BIG TIME

Chapter 27

Designing The Policy That Put Me In The Big Leagues

*My son Randy and I sat down
at the office and started designing
the policy, literally cutting
and pasting papers on a table.*

Losing Iowa State's big renewal checks gave me
all the motivation I needed; it was time to think
seriously about the Medicare supplement policy
I'd learned about at the convention. Unlike that
little company in Texas, I had access to nationwide
markets, and I knew we could do something
big with it. My son Randy and I sat down at the
office and started designing the policy, literally
cutting and pasting papers on a table. We took
bits and pieces from other contracts and put them
together, adding our ideas. When we'd get a draft
done, we'd run across the street to the printer and
get good copies made. We'd check it over, change

some more, and print it again. When we finally got it finished, the contract was four pages long. Looking back, it's amazing that's all there was to a document that changed my life.

Continental was an insurance broker, but it wasn't an insurance company, and we needed a big one to underwrite the policy. I decided to approach several and see where I could get the best offer. I was still working with Atlantic American and its sister company, Bankers Fidelity, so I decided to talk with them first, essentially as a trial run. I knew they were going to be at an industry convention at the Don CeSar, a big old pink hotel right on the ocean in St. Petersburg, just twenty miles south of my condo in Clearwater, and I set up an appointment with the presidents of both Atlantic American and Bankers Fidelity.

I just knew this thing could earn a lot of money. How much was anybody's guess, but I needed figures as part of the pitch I was making. I kind of pulled the numbers out of the air—$20 to $30 million sounded good—and that's what I put down as the amount of premiums we could be bringing in within a few years.

I didn't take Atlantic American all that seriously because I thought the numbers would scare them to death. I figured it was more than they'd want to take on, since they weren't a huge company, so I wasn't all that fired up. In fact, I started my presentation at the hotel rather flat. I broke my own rule about being the most enthusiastic guy I could be. Randy and I showed them the policy and talked about the numbers I'd come up with. They perked up and started asking questions that showed me they were excited and taking it seriously. I could have kicked myself for not being more on fire about it, and right then I upped my level of enthusiasm.

What I didn't know was that the company had money they needed to do something with. My timing was perfect. These guys recognized this as a policy that had real legs, and they had the money to put in reserve to pay claims. As we ended the meeting, it looked like we had a deal.

I had my attorney draft a contract with all the features I wanted. It would give me 75 percent of the premium the first year, 25 percent the second, and 20 percent thereafter. Those are terrific splits, the kind you just can't get anymore. I would give the agents and agencies who sold the policies the bulk of that, but it gave me room to do very well. Given the splits, I knew Atlantic American would have to run a really tight ship in order to earn enough money in the long run, but I thought I'd give it a try. They could try to negotiate a better deal if they wanted. I sent the contract to them, and they resisted at first, but I put pressure on them over the next couple of weeks and they came around. I went down to Atlanta for the signing.

Jack Featherstone, a general agent who represented the company and was a good friend, was visiting Nashville at the time. He knew about this contract and how much I wanted it. When I drove back to town after the signing, I went by the motel where he was staying. I pulled into the parking lot, blowing the horn. Jack came out on the balcony on the second floor, and I jumped out of the car. I threw that contract up in the air, hollering, "I got it done!"

Atlantic American and Bankers Fidelity—they operated in some states under one name, in others under the other—now had exclusive marketing rights for the policy. They could put their nationwide network of agents to work on leads, sell policies, and keep their percentage of the premiums. Of the 75/25/20 split, the average producers would get 55 percent the first year and 15 percent thereafter, giving me 20 percent the first year, 10 the second, and 5 thereafter. The highest I'd pay out—and this was to superagents, real producers who had long histories with me—would be 70/20/15, which would give me 5 percent of anything they sold. Atlantic American would get about 25 percent of the first year's premiums and more after that.

The premiums themselves were low, so the customers were getting a great deal on a good, solid Medicare supplement. That made it attractive to agents, and I knew the bottom line to success was having a policy that agents wanted to sell.

Recruiting agents involved a little sleight of hand because they knew I had designed this policy and was marketing it through Atlantic American, and I knew there would be some jealousy. It's just human nature. Some of them would want to deal with Atlantic American rather than Continental's Nashville office, thinking that would keep some of the money out of my pocket. It didn't. In May of 1983, we opened a small Atlanta office, even making sure it was in the same zip code as Atlantic American, to give agents an alternative. We mailed out brochures to prospective agents that said "Atlantic American" and listed the Atlanta address and an 800 number, but it was still us. Many agents thought they were going around me and getting a better deal if they dealt with that office, and we didn't mind if they thought that.

The satellite office really served us well, but we couldn't seem to find anyone qualified to head it up permanently. We kept someone there to ship contracts, brochures, applications, and other supplies out of the office so they came from Atlanta, but finally we just had calls forwarded to the Nashville office, since 90 percent of our business was done on the phone anyway.

Those calls, mostly from agents, went to my director of marketing. He'd even keep up with the weather in Atlanta so he could drop it into the conversation. He brought a lot of big agents on board, including a guy who owned his own plane and wanted to fly to the "home office" for a meeting. Our marketing director figured he'd better make it look good, so he went to Atlantic American's headquarters and found an executive who let him use his office. The agent flew in, and the marketing director was waiting for him in a great-looking Atlanta office. It took the guy a couple of years to figure out he was under the CIS managing general contract, but he was earning enough money that when he did, he just laughed about it.

A lot of people were earning enough money not to worry about appearances. We had the best policy, the best rates, and the highest commissions of anybody anywhere, and did we ever kick ass! People who didn't know me before knew me then— to this day, I'm known all over the country for that Atlantic American deal. Money was pouring in. We had the hottest product on the market, and everybody wanted to sell it. The first year, we did $3 million worth of business. The second year, it was $8 million, and we bought our first computers to help us keep up with the influx. As state insurance departments signed off on the policy and it came on line in more and more states, and as agents saw what they could earn on it, it really took off. I'd go into a state and recruit the largest agency there, and it would recruit all its agents, who could number in the hundreds. That meant other people were doing what I used to have to do—recruit individual agents. That's what let us grow so fast. I had just about every big marketer in the country representing me, as well as a little army of small agents. The third year we did $44 million in new sales, and in the fourth year it was $67 million. By 1986, I had more than ten thousand agents in seventeen states licensed, and Continental was earning $10 million. My overwrite check ran to more than $600,000 a month. We were in the big time. My estimate of $20 to $30 million as the amount we could sell yearly way undersold what we accomplished. We had doubled that in just three years.

I was in the big leagues in other ways as well. In 1979, Belmont College, which became Belmont University in 1991, asked me to serve on its board of directors. I can't begin to say how honored I felt. I had dropped out of high school, then earned my diploma through the mail, and now I was being asked to become part of a college board. Belmont has been part of Nashville's educational system since 1890, and I had taken interest in it almost by accident. The home Sadie and I lived in on Acklen Avenue was just down the street from Belmont—the mansion and grounds that became the school were originally owned by Adelicia Acklen—and as I drove by in those days I couldn't help but notice the peeling paint and other signs of an institution that could use a little more care. When they asked, I gladly said yes.

Then in 1983, I decided to establish a scholarship. I wanted to help the student who wanted to help himself or herself, and I could picture the money going to someone working his or her way through school who could really use a hand. I put up $50,000, but I was doing so well at the time that I began feeling cheap, and so I doubled it and gave $100,000. I've been adding to it just about every year since.

I'll never forget the very first batch of thank-you letters I got. I had been working hard, and my desk had gotten stacked up, so one night I decided to stay and clean up my in basket. I dictated letters and memos, and around 8:00 p.m., I reached the bottom and came across six or seven letters from students thanking me. Reading how important their education was to them and how grateful they were for the help made me really emotional. Through the years I've gotten a lot of letters like that, and I've read and treasured every one.

I felt like I was on a new level of personal giving as well. There were many other times when I saw opportunities to be helpful and took them. One year I saw in the paper where a house had burned down. One of the children died in the fire, and the family was really destitute. I clipped the story, and when Randy came into my office, I said, "Here's a family I want to help this year. Call this reporter and see if you can get a phone number."

I called and talked to the woman and found out they didn't have anything. I said, "Could you use a stove? Do you need a table and chairs?" She said yes to both, so I took a stove and a table and chairs from my mother-in-law's basement, then called a bunch of friends.

"If you've got anything you're not using," I told them, "and can give it away to a family whose house is burned out, let me know." They all pitched in, and I hooked a trailer to our motor home and packed it full of stuff. I picked up my friends Don and Joyce Wolfe, and we bought groceries and toys for all the kids. The family lived way up on the other side of Woodbury, and as we passed through Murfreesboro, Don said, "Pull in here. I want to buy these two boys a bicycle." I told them what we were doing, and the man said, "I'd give you the bicycles, but I've exceeded what I'm supposed to do for charity this year, so I'll give them to you for half price." It's always warmed my heart to see people who will contribute in a case like that.

The family lived back in the country, and we were crossing bridges I wasn't sure would hold. I didn't think we'd ever find the place, but finally, about 8:30 p.m. on Christmas Eve, we got there. We started bringing that stuff in, and when we brought the stove in, the woman just lit up. I handed her several hundred dollars in cash that I and some others had put together, and she was as grateful as she could be. It was another one of those great moments.

Chapter 28

Continental Life Center—My Dream Building

*"All I know to tell you is
I didn't know it couldn't be done."*

I was always looking to expand the business. Marketing was my specialty—finding the big agencies, the ones I knew could sell a lot of policies, and convincing them that ours was a great product to have. I had never lost the confidence— call it cockiness if you like—that I had as a young salesman. I knew my odds were good when I went to talk to someone.

I was driving once to our family's condo in Clearwater, and I stopped in Atlanta to visit the president of Atlantic American, as I always did.

"I'm going to go to the condo to relax for a few days," I told him, "and then I'm going to go over and recruit the National Health Agency."

He laughed. "I'll bet you do," he said.

"Now, do you understand what I said? I'm going to go to the condo for a few days, and then I'm going to recruit National Health. I might need you to come down and help me close. Can you do that?"

"Yeah," he said. "I can come down."

It would be good for Atlantic American, too, since they'd be getting their commission.

I had lunch with a few of National Health's key people, and they liked what they saw. We spent two hours talking over the contract, and then I called Atlantic American's president and told him to come down the next day. We all got together and settled on the contract.

I drove him back to the airport, and for the longest time he didn't say a word. Finally he said, "If they do what they say they're going to do, and I don't doubt but what they will, you just earned ten thousand dollars a month."

"Not a bad day's work, is it?" I said.

"I'm in the wrong end of this business," he said.

The trouble over the long haul was, as I suspected, that Atlantic American, which had tighter margins, wasn't earning enough of a percentage as they sold my policies. I believe they could have made that work, but they were compounding the problem on two fronts, probably because they didn't have enough experience with that kind of policy.

First, they passed up a strategy I suggested right up front to help retain business. Another company I'd worked with had a prelapse conservation program that I told Atlantic American about. A couple of weeks after someone bought a policy, we'd send out a letter congratulating them on their choice. We'd send similar letters and brochures—just goodwill stuff, really—a couple of times a year. The company had done a study on it. For two years, they sent out those mailings to people whose policies were issued on even-numbered days but not to those whose policies were issued on odd-numbered days. They found that those who got the letters were 11 to 14 percent more likely to renew. They knew it worked. I knew it worked. I knew it would be a good thing for Atlantic American to do, and I offered it to them, complete with color brochures. Yes, it cost money, but I figured anything that helped you retain an extra 11 to 14 percent of your business was worth it. They thought it was too expensive and turned it down.

Then they didn't manage their agents well enough, so they ended up paying excess commission on top of what we were getting. I tried to warn them up front about that too. The agents would in essence rewrite their own business, coming back a year or two down the road and updating or amending a policy they'd sold earlier. That should have been handled as a conversion, but the company didn't have any more sense than to allow it as new business and pay that commission all over again. I could see it happening, but they wouldn't listen to me.

In the meantime, the money rolled in, and I had to do something with it. Practically speaking, our biggest need at the time was office space. We were feeling cramped in our offices on Nolensville Road, and I knew it was time to trade up. I also knew what a big, long-term commitment real estate was.

We checked around and found a 2.6-acre lot in Brentwood, an upscale suburb south of Nashville, and talked with builders about the kind of building we needed. We were talking $3 to $4 million, a huge commitment at that point in my life. Just the thought of it made me nervous. It might be better to lease, since I was worried we might end up with a white elephant. I talked to people inside and outside the company and wrestled with it for a good year. Insurance I understood. This was an area I didn't know. All in all, I've never put more thought into a decision than I put into that one.

Finally, one morning I woke up with the green light. My subconscious, as it always does when I do the right amount of research and thinking, worked it out for me while I was asleep. When that happens, I go do it. And that's just what I did. I had the cash to pay for it outright, but my accountant told me to look at financing.

"You don't want to put your money in that building," he said. There was a government program that would make any loan I got essentially tax-free. It had to be done by December, and this was November. I started talking to banks, saying I wanted $2.5 million, and soon Third National and First Tennessee were bidding against each other. I had such good credit that their bids actually got below the prime rate. I was earning more than that on the money I had in the bank, so I would have been losing money to use my own. I was in Atlanta when the man from First Tennessee called me.

"I can give you the money at 67 percent of prime," he said. "You can have that if you'll take it now."

"If you can offer that, you've got the deal," I said. "I won't even go back to Third National."

"You've got it," he said.

Through the years, people have asked me, "How in the world did you get that rate?" I said,

"All I know to tell you is I didn't know it couldn't be done."

I asked the city of Brentwood to rename the street we were building on to Continental Way, and they did. I got really involved in designing that building, thinking about what we needed and how it should be laid out. I carried that structure and the people who would be working in it around in my head while the site itself was nothing more than flat ground.

Early in 1986 we moved in, taking up about half of the building's forty-thousand square feet. The rest I rented out.

The open house we held to celebrate the opening of The Continental Life Center was memorable for a couple of reasons. First, it was a $30,000 party, with a big tent out front, a piano player, shrimp and other hors d'oeuvres, and escorts to take six hundred people through the building. I remember stopping to take out my handkerchief to polish the brass on one of the elevators because I didn't think it had been cleaned well enough and I wanted our guests to see a first-class operation in every detail. Second, I got a monetary surprise. I was writing so much business that the Georgia Department of Insurance had gone in to make sure we didn't have any inappropriate ties to Atlantic American. Then Atlantic American's chairman had a special audit done on my account. The audit disclosed that they had miscalculated my premiums and actually owed me more money. They sent a representative to the open house with a statement and a check for $16,000, which paid for more than half the party.

It was just indicative of the way that money was flowing out of Atlantic American's Atlanta headquarters. Once that started, they poured millions into the company to keep it afloat. Besides the double-dip commissions, they were paying me my percentage on rate increases, which is not something a company should ordinarily do, but which was part of our agreement. They called me in and asked if I would take that out of the contract. I knew they were in a tight spot, and so I agreed. It probably cost me several million dollars, but I knew it had to be done to save this big block of business I had with them.

Even so, we experienced a problem common to many policies. We were forced into larger and larger rate increases, and finally the program began to fall apart and the amount of business they wrote on the policy began to fade. It had been a great ride. That policy made my name on a much bigger national scale, brought in millions and millions of dollars, and let me launch my own company, Continental Life Insurance Company of Brentwood, Tennessee.

Chapter 29

Continental Life Insurance Co.— My Dream Company

*Unless you set other, bigger goals,
even success can get stale
and turn into failure.*

I had dreamed of starting my own insurance company and competing with the big boys as far back as 1978. In fact, I once said as much in my column for the Continental newsletter. At the time, the chairman of Atlantic American saw it and alerted his marketing company, essentially telling them to keep an eye on me.

I actually founded the company in 1983, although I didn't really do much with it for several years—I was too busy cashing checks from Atlantic American. Still, founding it was another big turning point in my career. I knew the kind of policies I wanted to offer. I knew what other companies were doing right and what they were doing wrong; after all, I had been watching them for twenty-five years. Now I wanted a platform for selling my own products. I wanted to write policies I knew would work and compete with the companies I'd been representing all these years. I had the money to start it, the willingness to work hard, and access to a lot of agents. And I knew that unless you set other, bigger goals, even success can get stale and turn into failure.

One of the ways to start an insurance company is to buy an existing charter from a company that's no longer active. In some cases, those are companies that got in financial trouble one way or another. I looked at several of them, and the people in the Tennessee Department of Insurance warned me off them, in one case saying, "Look, I can't go into a lot of detail about this, but you don't want that one."

I decided just to go ahead with a new charter. My lawyer, Bill Bradley, had pretty much grown up in the insurance business. His dad had founded the Hermitage Health and Life Insurance Company and run it for many years. Bill had all the knowledge and experience I needed. He and I went to the commissioner's office and spent an hour hammering out details. As we were walking down the hall afterward, Bill said, "Let me shake your hand. I have just witnessed twenty-five years' reputation working for you. I've represented a lot of people, and I have never seen anything like it. That insurance department is absolutely knocking itself out trying to help you get that company started. It's something I've never seen before, and it tells me one thing—they believe in Randall Baskin." It was a good feeling.

There were just a few final steps, and it occurred to me that it would be great to make the announcement of the new company at our annual awards banquet, which was scheduled for the following night, a Friday. I called the commissioner's office and said, "Is there any chance we could get this done by tomorrow night?"

"Well," the commissioner said, "before we can issue the license, you've got to have the money in the bank, and I've got to send an inspector out to verify it. I'll tell you what. If you can make the deposit today, I'll send the inspector out in the morning, and we can have you chartered tomorrow afternoon."

I told Shirley Felts, my secretary, "Get the checkbook and let's go." She actually wrote the check, for $1,125,000, in the car on the way to the bank. To this day, that check, shaky handwriting and all, sits in a case in my office.

They sent a representative to the bank the next morning, then called and told me that the license had been issued and that I could come by and pick it up. Friday night at the banquet, I shocked everybody by announcing that I had just chartered a new insurance company—Continental Life Insurance Company of Brentwood, Tennessee. It would be owned by Continental Insurance Service, Inc.

Among the things Napoleon Hill learned in studying success was that most men who are very successful hit stride in their fifties, and that was the case with me. When I founded Continental, I was fifty-one years old. It seems like it takes that much time to accumulate the experience, the trial-and-error wisdom, and the vision to undertake big enterprises. When I finally put my full effort into Continental Life, beginning in 1987, it was with a wealth of knowledge at my disposal. I drew heavily on what I'd seen other companies do. Bankers Service Life, for example, handled all its business really well, and I compared what I did to what they did. If it lined up, I was on the right track, since they had the money and the actuaries to do things right. When it came to designing policies, I learned from the mistakes made by Atlantic American. I didn't want a policy that was too good to the agents at the expense of either the company or the policyholder.

What I wanted was a company that was win-win-win. I wanted the agents, the policyholders, and our company all to benefit from our design. My number one goal was to offer the best deal possible for the insured over the long haul—period. I wanted good, solid policies with reasonable premiums. That would be good for policyholders and for us—happy customers spread the word. It would let the agents sell more and would help us get a good return on our investment. Then I'd strive to have the smallest rate increases and the fastest, most efficient payment on claims of anybody. The thing you really have to sell is your service. That's what builds a company's reputation—does it pay off when you file a claim? If you can beat your competition there, you win, and that's what I set out to do. It was the fulfillment of that section of Napoleon Hill's *Think and Grow Rich* that I recited every day, the part summed up by the line, "I will engage in no transaction which does not benefit all whom it affects." That was the foundation on which I'd build Continental Life.

My first policy was a variation on the Medicaid supplement I marketed through Atlantic American. I knew this kind of policy had its share of risks. That's why the variation I had, where benefits wouldn't exceed those of Medicare, was so important. Still, I'd seen Atlantic American lose control of the process by not policing their agents well. I'd have to do a better job of that.

Above all, I had to control the underwriting, the process by which you assess what kind of risk you're undertaking. I had to know whether the potential policyholder was healthy. What was the likelihood that he or she would face an illness or accident that would cost the company money? I had watched other companies mishandle that process over and over. They'd sign somebody up they shouldn't have, then rescind the policy when the claim came in. It amounted to qualifying the prospect at claim time. I couldn't stand that. It was a surefire way to kill a company's reputation.

The application is designed to help a company gather the necessary information. Once in a while you get people lying on them, but that isn't often. Usually the problem is that the company is lax or the agents provide incomplete or erroneous information, leaving out details that would throw up a red flag. I couldn't let either happen. First, I wanted agents who wouldn't hide health problems, who would recognize and bring up potential difficulties right up front. Then, I decided to do something that was a check on both the applicant and the agent—I would have someone in-house follow up on applications and qualify the policyholder by phone.

It just so happened that one of the people who applied for that job was an out-of-work nurse. It didn't take long to realize she fit the bill perfectly. She knew what to ask. She understood the medications that people were taking. She could pick up on things others would miss and know when we should check back with an applicant's doctor.

The job market was such that there were several other nurses this woman knew who were available, and I hired them too. It was unheard of to use phone calls, to say nothing of nurses, to help underwrite in the Medicare supplement industry, but tightening this part of the process meant that when a claim came in, we could just go ahead and pay it.

The flip side was that the underwriting was so strict the agents started balking. There were a lot of potential customers who couldn't meet our underwriting requirements, so the agents were losing sales. If there was anything the least bit questionable, we would check it out. Our nurses called every applicant and went over every line with a microscope. If we caught an agent deliberately withholding or falsifying something, we'd terminate him, and it didn't take many for the others to get the message. The word spread fast. Other companies would tolerate that. We wouldn't. Pretty soon we started hearing from agents.

"Randall," they'd say, "we love you to death, but we can't put up with your underwriting."

In fact, quite a few salesmen left. There were other policies they could sell without worrying that their customers weren't going to pass muster. Production fell quite a bit. We struggled on that front for two years. I held on because I knew the only way I could hold rate increases down was to make sure I was insuring reasonably healthy people at the start. Then my marketing guy came to me and told me in detail just how much of a hit we were taking, and I started having second thoughts. *Maybe I should relax my underwriting*, I thought.

But that night I didn't sleep well, and when I

woke up, I said, "No. I'm not going to back off. I know I'm doing it right."

I went back to my marketing guy.

"I'm going to stick to my guns," I told him.

He was fit to be tied, but it was my company and we kept things the way they were.

It wasn't ninety days later that I had the development I needed. The competition began announcing rate increases that ranged as high as 30 percent. Mine averaged 7 percent. People who'd bought policies with the competition didn't renew. The agents' renewal checks plummeted as those companies lost business. What's more, those companies were only getting those big rate increases because the state insurance departments that had to approve them knew they were losing their shirts.

On the other hand, the agents selling my policies saw their checks grow. It didn't take them long to figure out who really had the better approach. If you hold your rate increases down and give outstanding claim service, you keep the business. They knew that satisfied customers mean referrals and bigger renewal checks. Suddenly the agents who'd been out selling other policies started running back to me.

"Randall," they said, "you're the only guy out there who knows what he's doing!"

That was the turning point. Those agents were suddenly very willing to go along with our underwriting. In fact, they started doing the job for us. If they were talking to someone they knew we wouldn't take, they would send the business to another company. It wasn't long before I became the primary company for a lot of agents. Win-win-win was a reality, and we were off and running.

Family was a bigger part of the picture than ever as we earned that success through the 1980s. Once Roger earned his B.A. in business administration from MTSU, he came to work for me full-time. He spent six or eight months in the field, with Marion taking him out and showing him the ropes, but he never did like it. He was nowhere near as outgoing as Randy was, and he was pretty tenderhearted. It was tough for him to close a sale, especially if the people were old or not doing very well financially. He'd get to feeling sorry for them, and he'd want to pay their premiums.

In 1986 I made him agency secretary, a job he held for quite a while. He put together our newsletter and the monthly *Pacesetter*. I'd choose inspirational bits and maybe write a column, and he'd pull together the sales numbers and handle the editing, graphics, layout, and printing.

Randy was vice president of marketing at the time and we traveled a lot together. I tried to get him and Roger pumped up about the inspirational reading I did, but they both turned up their noses at it. Finally one day on a plane trip Randy opened up to me. He said that both he and Roger felt intimidated by me. I came across as so strong and so successful that they knew they never had a chance of achieving what I had. It was tough to live in my shadow. The reading I had done was just part of it. I guess they heard far more about it than they wanted to listen to.

That discussion did affect the way I thought about things, but it didn't change much. They had both been part of the business since childhood. They always felt like they knew where they were going to work, but in some sense that was all it was—a place to work. They never bought into the founding vision, the drive for success I had. The success was already in place, and they didn't feel like they had a piece of it.

When the father is the head of the company and family members work there, it's tough on both the business and the personal sides. That was true everywhere I looked. Marion and his wife worked for me. Sadie, Randy, and Roger all worked for me. Both their wives worked for me. I always felt like the big bad wolf. I would tell them going in, "You're supposed to set the example, because if you goof off, everybody will be looking at you. If you can get away with it, that helps define our family."

They would listen, and I'm sure they had good intentions, but it's human nature that they would take advantage of the situation, and sure enough they would drift off course from time to time. When they did, I'd come down hard on them. Then, any tension that resulted from that would slop over and make itself felt at parties and family events. Everybody I've ever talked to who's had a family business says the same thing.

When I walked in that front door at the home office, I was a different person. I was Mr. Continental Insurance, all business. People respect you for being that way. They follow you because they see you're the kind of leader who does what he asks of people. That's how I developed good, loyal people— they had respect for me.

The hours I put in were determined by what I had going on, although I never did back off much. I've always been a workaholic. I tried to get that over to Marion and Cecil, Randy and Roger. "How much do you think about your job when you're not working?" I'd ask. "If you don't spend a reasonable amount of time thinking about your job, planning what you're going to do, then you're not into it."

That's how I did it, anyway. I would wake up at 2:00 or 3:00 in the morning and lie there and think about something.

"I thought we were tired," Sadie might say after we'd been somewhere and I'd be up before 5:00 to work on an article for the newsletter or a marketing plan. I do my good thinking in the morning, and I'll lie there in bed and think about it until at some point I'm to go out and get it on paper.

I should say that I never came down quite as hard on my family members as I might have on other employees. Sometimes to keep the peace I'd compromise and give a lot more latitude than I ever thought I would. I guess in the long run it was easier that way.

Chapter 30

A Loss That Never Heals

There are no words to describe just how broken the news left us.

Until 1991, I thought I was a man of steel. I had achieved a great deal of success in business and in life. I was running my own company. Sadie and I had come from poverty to wealth, and we were happy together. We had two sons who were part of my business, and although our relationship wasn't perfect, we were close and I was proud of them. But in November of that year, I learned I was simple flesh and blood, as susceptible to the awful arrows of tragedy and heartache as anyone.

It was the Sunday before Thanksgiving, and Sadie and I were at our farm in Giles County, about an hour south of Nashville, with Marion and Dot. We bought it as a getaway, and we spent many wonderful days there, riding horses or four-wheelers, talking and laughing with friends into the night, and just enjoying life. Marion and I were in the woods hunting squirrels, and Sadie and Dot were at the farmhouse.

We heard a four-wheeler hurrying toward us, and as it got close, we saw that it was Jack Featherstone, who lived across the street from the farm—he's the reason we found it in the first place. His exact words are a blur, but I can still remember the instant pit of anguish and despair in my stomach. Randy had been in a car wreck. He'd been killed.

Marion and I ran toward the house, and at one point I just fell to the ground, crying, overwhelmed by the pain and heartbreak of it. I lay there for several minutes until finally I got up and went on, knowing I had to go tell Sadie. But when I walked in, her tears told me that she had already gotten the call.

There are no words to describe just how broken the news left us. The son we'd had as teenagers, just as we were beginning our lives in that leaky trailer, poor but happy, the son whose sickness kept us up nights, the boy who put flyers on cars with Marion and me, the young man who grew up and went to college and made my company a true family business, the grown man who now had three sons of his own, was gone. He had been driving his Chevrolet Jimmy on Mack Hatcher Boulevard, and he swerved to avoid a car stopped at an intersection. His vehicle flipped over, and he was thrown partially through the moon roof and killed instantly. He wasn't wearing his seat belt.

The day before the funeral, with everyone gathered at the funeral home, I called the family together in a side room for a private meeting. I told them how proud I was that Randy was a Christian.

"This is a time when our faith in God is very

important," I said. "None of us can understand why this happened, and we may never understand it. We need to have faith and try to learn from this experience. Randy was a good person, and maybe God allowed this to happen to draw us closer to Him and to each other."

I don't know how I ever would have gotten through it without my faith in my Lord and Savior Jesus Christ.

The morning of his funeral I woke up early and sat on the side of the bed. So much about him went through my mind. I thought about the joy he'd brought us. I thought about the teenage scrapes he'd gotten into. No matter what he'd gotten into, in the end he was happy and proud to be part of our family, and we were stronger and better for it. I thought about the night at our place on Darlington when he told me how proud he was that I was his dad. I thought about the fact that he'd been saved, and I didn't need to worry about where he was going. I wanted to say something at his service, and I picked up a pen and a tablet beside the bed and just let what I was thinking and feeling flow onto the paper.

Sadie and I dressed and went on to the funeral. I had never seen so many flowers. At that time, it was the largest service ever held at the Woodbine Funeral Home. My good friend, the Reverend Paul Durham, handled the service. He asked if I was going to get up to read what I had prepared that morning, but I was so emotional I just couldn't do it.

I wrote:

Love is God's greatest gift that we will ever know on this earth. Some forty-one years ago, God gave Sadie and me our firstborn son, Randy Baskin. In those early years, at the age of eighteen, when just the necessities of life were a struggle, it was love that kept us together and it was love for one another that caused us to pull together.

Little did we know then that God included with this firstborn son, Randy, such a bundle of love. We thank God for that. We thank God for the forty-one years, eleven months, and twenty days we had Randy to love. We thank God for the love that he gave Randy and his great ability to radiate his love to everyone. We thank God for the love Randy had for his wife, Tammy, his three sons, Rafe, Blake, and Stefan, his brother Roger, his mother, and me.

My son Randy Baskin was a free giver of love. He loved everyone, and we thank God for his love he shared with all of us.

I felt like I'd been hit below the belt. Losing a child is probably the worst thing that can happen to a person, and I didn't handle it very well. It dampened my spirit a great deal. I've seen other people in similar situations come to accept it and go on. I look back and say, "Why didn't I do that?"

But it was too big and powerful for me to handle.

That farm and the hollow it sat in were never the same. Even our little Yorkie, who was normally always playful, got in the car when we first drove back to Nashville and just curled up. It was a long time before she'd rip and romp like she'd always done. Randy's in-laws came down that next week to celebrate Thanksgiving, which we always did at the farm, and we went through the motions, but it was a sad, sad time. It changed how we felt about Thanksgiving from then on.

I had just helped Randy buy a house that now he would never move into. I encouraged Tammy to take their three boys and move in, and a little later I voided the note I was holding on the house so they would have a home free and clear of debt. Tammy still lives there.

Two things happened in the weeks after Randy's death that I'll never forget. First, I remembered what that fortune-teller had told Sadie all those years ago—that I would become wealthy and we would have two sons, one of whom something would happen to. After all those years, I was amazed how she'd hit it on the head.

And two weeks after Randy's funeral, I was due to speak at a service at Radnor Baptist. I didn't feel much like talking, but I knew I needed to. My faith was sustaining me, and I was going to speak about a prime example of the way I put my faith into action. Back in the late 1970s I headed the bond committee that would pay off the loan we took out to build the church auditorium. That Sunday, two weeks after Randy's funeral, I gave a talk called "The Joy of Giving," and at the end of the service I presented the church with a check paying off the remaining bond debt of $56,000. Paul went back and checked, and through the fifteen years we'd been paying it off, I had paid over half of the note.

Along with my faith, the thing that brought me through that terrible time was work. The worst thing I could have done would have been to stop. I don't know that I ever would have gotten started again. I kept contacting agents like I always had, and I kept putting out the newsletter every week, looking for inspirational bits to put in it. But underneath the continued motion, I really didn't accept what had happened. I left Randy's office, which was next to mine, just the way it was. I couldn't make myself clean it out. I guess some part of me thought, *He's coming back.* The days turned to weeks, then to months.

At one point a good friend talked to us. She lived on the hill behind us on Old Hickory Boulevard, and she had lost a child too. She said, "As you grieve over Randy, be careful, because Roger will resent it."

It wasn't something I had thought about, but it made sense. Our world was so upside down and we grieved so much that Roger had to be all but saying to us, "I'm still here. You've still got me. You need me and I need you." In that light, I could tell that he was feeling some resentment for the way Randy's death had stolen us from him. From then on, Sadie and I did our best to work through it better, and especially to be more appreciative of Roger when we were around him.

It was a year and a half before finally I went to work one morning and an inner voice told me to clean Randy's office. I got a box, went in, and started putting his things in it. Roger saw what I was doing and came to help. We got three boxes, one for personal things to take to Tammy, one for business things to leave at the office, and one for things I wanted to take home. I know the employees were glad to see me clean it out. I should have done it the day after he died, but I just couldn't.

In the months and years since, I've developed a nervous condition I still have. I trace the beginning of it to that time. Randy's death is one of the places in my life where I didn't do things the way I thought I should. I believe that you have to deal with events you can't control up front—just face them and go on the best you can, which I didn't do very well. I'd have been much better off had I accepted it much sooner than I did. His loss still hurts, but Sadie and I are grateful for the time we had with him and the chance to share his love for as long as we did.

Chapter 31

Growing With Confidence

"You know more about the business than any man I've ever dealt with and you do it the right way."

By the early 1990s, CIS and CLI offered sixty health and life products between them, but most of what we sold—I'd say 90 percent or so— were Medicare supplement policies. By then, those policies had been standardized by federal regulation. There were several variations, each with specified benefits—any company's "Plan F" policy would look the same. The policies were easy to sell, and money rolled in. I was hiring agents left and right, and they were earning money just like we were. Their renewals increased faster than they had ever seen. It got to where I was sending quite a few guys monthly renewal checks in the $40,000 to $50,000 range, and one, Larry Franklin, was nearing $90,000. I was proud of that fact.

Larry was a good friend and a great example of how a person's fortunes can change drastically.

When I met him in the late 1970s, he was in his early thirties, working for National Health, the agency in St. Petersburg that sold a lot of my Atlantic American policy. Ten years later, in 1987, he called and said he'd had a disagreement with the owner and had been fired. I could tell how down and out he felt, and I invited him to visit me in Nashville, reimbursing him for his plane ticket. He's a nice guy with a lot of talent, and I wanted to make sure he didn't give up on insurance.

I spent the day with him and did my best to motivate him. "One day," I said, "you'll look back on this and see that it's the best thing that ever happened to Larry Franklin. Larry, you're a good man. You just weren't in the right situation. You need to go out there and build something for yourself. With your knowledge of the business, there's nothing that should keep you from doing just that."

He took a job with another company and did really well. Even the man who had fired him took a contract with him. Then that man died, and his widow asked Larry if he'd come back and help run the agency. When she decided to sell, Larry was able to buy it—with a lot of the money coming from what he was earning in overwrites on that contract with the former owner, the man who had fired him.

In June 1993, I called and asked him to fly to my office with his attorney to hammer out a contract so he could sell my policies. He and his attorney and me and my attorney sat down, and he handed me a contract he'd prepared as a starting point. I read it over and said, "This is the fairest contract I've ever seen, and I am going to sign it just as presented." He told me later that he had copied it from one of my contracts.

It wasn't long before he became my number one general agent. Through the years, Larry brought in more sales for Continental Life than anyone.

"You know," he told me years later, "none of this would have happened if it hadn't been for Randall Baskin believing in me when I didn't believe in myself. That talk gave me the courage to go out and try to make something happen." He always gave me a lot of credit for his success through the years, and it's always felt good.

Most of our top producers said Continental was the best-run company they'd ever represented. I took the good things the agents were saying about us and began to use them in our brochures.

"I've represented a lot of companies," said one, "and I've never represented a company where my renewals grew so fast. When they buy Continental, they keep Continental."

Over the years, I accumulated a file folder full of statements like, "You know more about the business than any man I've ever dealt with and you do it the right way."

Even competitors who didn't like me couldn't say anything bad about the way we did business. Agents who walked away, unwilling to follow our guidelines, would come back and want to work for us. Those who understood what we were doing, who had learned their lessons, I would take on, and many of them became good agents for us. One salesman and I had a disagreement, and he got mad and quit. A year or so passed, and then out of the clear blue one day I got the nicest letter from him, telling me what a great company I had. You just never knew. I called him and thanked him for the note and told him if he ever wanted to come back and work for me, he could. Not long afterward, he was with my company again.

My main role with the company was still as a marketer. I put great people in charge of claims and underwriting, but marketing was something I liked and kept a hand in. I was always eager to put the word out there to agents and agencies, to bring people on board to sell our products. We had started business in Tennessee, adding Florida in 1987 and going on to add state after state, agency by agency, after that.

One of the tools I really valued was the company's convention. Especially in the early years of Continental Life, Continental Insurance Service was still selling a lot for other firms, so we were always invited to their conventions. I never understood why. It was like inviting the fox into the henhouse. I was looking for good agents, just like they were. Those conventions were the perfect chance to get to meet and sweet-talk someone whose name I'd run across as an up-and-coming super salesman. We picked up some of our best agents and agencies that way.

I made sure I was getting the other companies' newsletters so I knew who was selling a lot of insurance for them. They got smart enough to stop listing agents' addresses or even their hometowns, but it wasn't hard to track somebody down and then call and ask him if he'd consider adding my products to his portfolio. If I knew a guy was a hotshot producer, I wanted him selling my products, and I'd offer him the best commissions I had.

Gradually, we had six thousand agents representing us in thirty-five states, and they had confidence in us. I saw it. If agents bought insurance for themselves, it was Continental. If they bought for their mothers, it was Continental. I was always proud of the fact that whenever Continental was in the mix of companies handled by MGAs—managing general agents, who oversaw agencies—I could pull them over to us. They'd start out complaining about my underwriting, but when they saw how the renewals built, they always understood.

On the other hand, I was tough. If someone tried to take advantage of the company or tried to beat the company out of a commission or a sale, I was the meanest man he ever saw. I tried to head off that kind of potential conflict up front. For instance, I had a provision in my contract with agents that if you rolled a Continental policy into another company's, you had fourteen days to reinstate it with us, or I would charge you one annual premium. The "fast" guy couldn't stand it. The mediocre guy didn't like it. Both of them would raise a fuss about it.

"Well," I'd say, "are you planning on rolling it?"

"No."

"Well, if you're not going to roll it, it's not going to apply to you."

The good agent, on the other hand, loved it. He wasn't going to be doing that anyway.

Good agents, quick claims payments, low premiums—it was all working and people were copying us. Five years after I started the company as the only one doing telephone interviews as part of the underwriting process, most of the other companies were doing it too. They had to. I was simply out-earning them. For years the company was earning more money than companies seven or eight times our size. What we sold, we kept. People swore by us.

The ratings reflected the respect we had earned.

The big rating agency, A. M. Best Company, attached a grade to insurers' financial strength and their ability to meet their obligations to policyholders. We requested our first rating from Best in 1991, and I visited their headquarters in Oldwick, New Jersey, in the process. They gave us a B+ (very good) rating early in 1992. Two years later, we were informed we had moved up to a B++ rating. We wanted an A or better.

They gave two reasons why we weren't getting it. The first was our geographic concentration. Most of our business was in a handful of states in the Southeast, and they wanted to see national coverage. We were always pushing to expand our reach, adding a state or two at a time, but at first we had just a few agents in many states.

The second was the concentration of our business in Medicare supplement policies. We were down from our peak of 90 percent or so, but they still represented probably 80 percent of our business, and Best wanted to see more life, accident, and other policies in the mix.

We did our best. We designed applications that let you add other policies to a Medicare supplement sale without additional forms. We made it so people could pay multiple policies with a single check or bank draft. That made marketing and selling other coverage easier, but it still didn't drive the percentages much. We started running campaigns encouraging our agents to diversify, and we hired people specifically to sell life insurance, but I never found anybody who could sell enough to make a dent. The highest we could drive the "other policies" total to was 27 or 28 percent, and we couldn't hold that very long.

We never did get that A rating from A. M. Best,

and I'm convinced there was a third reason that was just as important: we weren't one of the big boys. We didn't have the kind of deep-pocket reserves our larger competitors had. I knew—and Best knew—we were on as solid a footing as any of them when it came to how well we'd handled claims so far. And sure enough, years later, when we sold the company to someone with deep pockets, Continental got that A.

We had a good reputation with the state insurance commission as well. In the report that came with one of our first audits, the commission made a really complimentary remark about the stability of the company.

I decided to go ahead and publish what they'd said in our newsletter. They were on the phone just after it came out, saying, "You can't use our statements in advertising! That's inside information!" I apologized and said I didn't know any better, but it sure felt good getting the word out there.

Chapter 32

Insurance Is Peace Of Mind

*We went out of our way
to keep the customers
who bought insurance with us.*

From the customer's standpoint, insurance is about peace of mind. It's about buying confidence. You hope you keep your good health, but if you get sick, you want to know you've got a policy from a reputable company that's agreed to pay your claim so you can get the treatment you need without incurring a financial burden.

It's hard to explain just how close someone who's had several sizable claims can feel toward the insurance company that's written those checks, the person on the other end of the phone, or the person who's written the letter from the home office. Straightening out a problem, giving prompt, efficient claim service, really wins people over. It means the world to someone who's been sick and suffering to get a notice that the doctor and the hospital have been taken care of.

We got a lot of letters from people telling us they didn't know what they would have done without us. That's what built Continental. I daresay we probably had the finest claims department in the country. Nobody beat us because we underwrote up front, so there were very few claims that we questioned. I reversed the process whereby so many companies underwrote at claim time and tried to find a reason not to pay. I tried to find a reason to pay those claims fast, and I do mean fast. The average time it took us to get a check out once we'd received the claim form was 4.7 days. To the best of my knowledge, no one else was even close, and that will build a reputation that separates you from other companies.

That kind of service and the loyalty it generated helped us as we sought new customers, which is one of the more expensive parts of doing business. There's the cost of the lead, travel, phone calls, administration, and paperwork, so you want to find policyholders who are going to stay, who will renew year after year. It became more and more important for us to encourage our agents to ask policyholders who were happy with their policies about other kinds of coverage—final expense, cancer protection, long-term care coverage—and to encourage them to refer their friends to us. We continued to look for customers wherever it made sense, advertising in places like the *Baptist and Reflector*, the news journal of the Tennessee Baptist Convention, but we knew the bottom-line importance of word of mouth.

We went out of our way to keep the customers who bought insurance with us. We did what I knew worked—we'd send them several letters in the first year, thanking them for the business, telling them how to make the most of their coverage, giving them information about the company, and a lot more.

That kind of attention won over agents too. A good agent wants to see his policyholders treated right, and he's got the right to question the company if it's not doing that. We paid so promptly that we always had great relations with our agents.

I would sit in on claims meetings where we reviewed cases, and I was probably bad for the bottom line. When there was a question, most of the time I would just tell the claims department to go ahead and pay it. I knew the company was earning money, and I felt like I could do more harm than good by finding a reason to withhold payment. Now, if a case looked like fraud was involved, that was different, but there were times when I knew it was simple ignorance or misunderstanding, and I wasn't going to punish them for that. We had a claim from a woman in her late seventies who was suffering from congestive heart failure. When we got her medical records, we found she'd been diagnosed with congestive heart failure before she'd applied for our policy and hadn't mentioned it. I called her myself, told her who I was, and asked her about her problems.

"How long have you realized you've had congestive heart failure?" I asked.

"What's that?" she said.

I explained what it was, and she said, "Well, I know I take something for my heart that my doctor prescribes."

I'm usually perceptive enough to know when people are being honest, and she was being honest. She didn't understand the term and hadn't reported it when she applied. Legally, that didn't make a difference—we could have rescinded the policy. But it made a difference to me, and I took her side. It would have been grossly unfair to her to take away her insurance.

"Your policy will remain in effect," I told her, "and I'll send you a check."

Rescinding a policy was a huge step. Chances are, people like her had a policy that would have covered whatever we were rescinding over and dropped it to apply for our policy. Our coverage was the key to making them decide to change. If I saw the policyholder knew what he was talking about, that was different, but overall I was pretty much against rescinding policies.

Because of that lady and others like her, I did instruct my telephone people to be sure they explained congestive heart failure during the underwriting follow-up call and to be sure they knew whether or not the person had it.

There were other times I got involved on that kind of level—I could be a pretty hands-on guy. A claim came in on another congestive heart failure case not long after we'd issued the policy—that was always a red flag—and it had come from an agent I wasn't sure I trusted yet. It looked suspicious, so I drove down to Pulaski to talk with the policyholder. I was going to rescind the insurance and fire the agent if it was what I thought it was.

Both the man and his wife were policyholders, and I asked the man about the agent and the application. We talked a while, and I couldn't see where they or the agent had done a thing wrong. I said we'd keep their policies in force. In fact, the woman had a lesser policy than her husband, and she asked if I could upgrade and I said yes.

I got back to the home office and told them what

had happened, and they laughed. One of my people said, "We don't need to be sending you out on cases. You'll break the company."

Fortunately, our financial situation was always such that I could afford to err on the side of payment. That was one of the advantages of the way I managed the company. Do the underwriting first, the way it should be done, and you've got a great head start. Yes, I had to raise premiums every year, but my increases were generally half or sometimes a third of what my competition's were.

That's not to say our claims ratio was low. It wasn't. State insurance departments wanted it in the 68 to 70 percent range, and that was one of the things they looked at when you applied for rate increases in the states where you were licensed to do business. Ours was generally in the high seventies or low eighties. We were paying out a lot. It worked because I was able to keep overhead low. I owned the building, and I wasn't taking much of a salary. For most of the years I ran Continental Life, I paid myself just $300,000.

I also drove a hard bargain for supplies. It was a skill I'd learned from my dad. I watched him wheel and deal and negotiate for all kinds of things when I was a kid, and I had always done that too. Once I could pay cash for cars and boats and homes, I drove the hardest bargains I could. "One offer is worth a dozen lookers," my dad used to tell me. "Always remember that." I did. Sadie used to hate to watch me cutting a deal for a car. I was a tough and patient negotiator, and she'd get mad at the way I kept digging for that rock bottom. She'd just go get in the car. Finally I'd give them the figure I was willing to pay and say, "Remember, this is a cash offer." Then I'd go get in the car myself and drive off if I had to. I had done my research. I had a friend who could tell me from the serial number how long the dealer had the car on the lot and that would tell me how desperate he might be to move it. I knew just how low I could go, and they'd always come around.

I carried that skill into the business. We updated our computers at one point in a deal that went well into six figures. Our operations vice president, who was dealing with the computer people, came to me and said, "I've beat these people down to where they aren't going to go any lower. I think we've got a pretty good price."

I met with them and in ten minutes got $10,000 more knocked off the price. Our VP was actually kind of mad about it.

"You told me that was the best price you could give us," he said to their salesman.

"Well," he said, "I guess the only thing I can tell you is that you're not the man in the corner office."

That happened with all our big purchases. Every time we bought furniture or anything large, they called me in at the end, and I had a way of saving us a little more. In fact, the guys in the company used to watch me operate just to see how I did it.

I wasn't that good when it came to rate increases. When it came time to apply to the states for them, our actuary worked from a formula that I could never understand to tell us what we should ask for. He also told me how much money I had to have in reserve.

"You'll be all right until your payouts get over this amount," he'd tell me, and when I neared that figure, he'd tell me, "You're getting close—put some more in," and I'd put another $1 or $2 or $3 million in reserves.

Still, our profit, like the profit of most insurance companies, was not all about claims and expenses versus premiums. No, profit was a matter of investment income, pure and simple, for most every insurance company, and that's what it was for us. We'd put money into AA and AAA securities, things like municipal bonds or bonds from Fannie Mae or Ginnie Mae.

Behind all the finances, giving the policyholder the best deal I could served us well. It must have been the right approach because, among other things, it kept us out of court. My attorney couldn't believe it.

"Most companies get stacks of lawsuits," he said to me once.

"Why would they sue me?" I said. "I pay them!"

When it came to policyholders, I remember just one lawsuit, and that was filed by a claim artist. He lived in California and bought a policy in Florida, then filed a claim for an extended hospital stay. We learned he had ten other plans that he had not reported on his application. We agreed to buy back the policy, which kept it out of court.

Once or twice an agent sued me in small claims court—disputes over a renewal or something else that didn't amount to more than a few hundred dollars—but those were just nuisance claims. I'd call the guy and pay him and just go on.

I also liked to remember that our policyholders were flesh-and-blood people, and now and then I would want to do something special for them. Someone brought to my attention that a policyholder named Louise Cunningham in Pulaski was turning one hundred. She'd taken out the policy eighteen years earlier, in 1987, and we'd paid quite a few claims on her. I said to my agency secretary, "Don't you think it would be nice to take her a cake?" He called and set it up, and when we showed up at her door with a birthday cake, she had her family and friends there and was dressed in her best outfit. We had a great talk with her— she'd stayed up the night before watching the Braves until the thirteenth inning when Chipper Jones hit a home run that won the game. The local newspaper sent a reporter, and she really did appreciate the gesture. Less than a year later she died. I was always glad we went to see her.

Chapter 33

Good Agents And Good Employees Make A Great Company

I never used motivational speakers at Continental Life. That was my job.

As head of my own company, it was up to me to oversee our annual conventions. I had to reward our bigger-producing agents, and I knew I had to treat them like stars. I tried to copy some of the things that Union Bankers had done—the limos and gifts and trips. I do have to admit that it was a lot more fun being on the receiving end of that sort of thing, but the fact that I could do that for agents meant they were doing well, which meant that the company and I were also doing well.

I had always looked for bigger and better ways

to reward the top sellers. I met a Dallas diamond wholesaler through one of our agents in Miami and had him send me diamond clusters. He'd send twenty or so a year, and I'd give seven or eight away to top salesmen, pay for those, and send the rest back. The agents loved them, and I got a lot of mileage out of that connection. Then I bought two condos in Panama City, Florida—one for me and one for the company. I'd let the agents win trips down there, and I made a deal with a nearby restaurant. They had a six-inch-thick filet they named the Baskin special, and the agents who won the trip could eat whatever they wanted at the restaurant on me, and they almost always ate the Baskin special. It was something they'd really compete for.

I loved celebrating with long-time producers and friends. Late in the game, in 2005, I was able to honor Siegel Heffington with the Continental Life Chairman of the Board's Award. He and I had started out with Bankers Service about the same time. He was in Oklahoma, and he was always the leader in life insurance sales like I was in health insurance sales. We stayed friends through the years, and when Continental Life got licensed in Oklahoma, thirty years after we met, he was the first person I thought of. He was a good salesman and a hard worker, and he liked a nice paycheck and the lifestyle that went with it. That's always a good combination, and I wanted him on my team. He took a contract and started selling and brought in a lot of business for us over the years. Siegel was a loner who could outsell three or four average agents. He was never part of an agency, but he'd been in the business so long and was so well thought of in Oklahoma that he had a huge pool of people to draw from.

He won a lot of prizes and trips, and I remember on one of them standing with him on the balcony of my condo in Florida. "I've been at this a long time," he said, "and I've represented a lot of companies. Nobody I've represented did it the way you have. You've earned your success the right way. You hold your premiums down and still pay your claims promptly. You pay your agents fast, and the renewals are always great. When I call the girls in your office, they're always friendly, and they take care of whatever I need right away. I just want you to know I'm proud of you."

Coming from him, that was the greatest compliment I could have gotten. It really meant a lot to me.

Not long afterward I heard he'd gotten cancer, and he died shortly after that. He was part of a generation of good guys that I'd grown up with in the insurance business.

Another guy I liked doing business with was Charlie DuBose, who was in business with his son Bubba in South Carolina. Charlie was a great guy whose family had been in the business since 1928, and he and I got to be friends. We were both selling for Union Bankers, and every now and then he'd beat me for a month and I'd never hear the end of it.

One day after I started Continental Life, I pulled up to his little office in my big old Prevost motor coach. I showed him what I had to offer, and he took a contract to sell my policies. He sent me a few applications and liked the way we handled them, so he sent a few more. The first thing you know, he was sending me a lot of business, and it wasn't long before I became his primary carrier.

That's the way I liked to do business, offering a

good product and having quality people like Charlie selling it. I look at that as doing things the right way. Quality people, the best people, are out there, and they're the ones you want. They're not harder to get—in fact, they're easier to get, but you've got to deal with them on their own terms and you've got to sell yourself to them. You've got to convince them to buy you as well as your product. They want the absolute best, just like you do. They've got customers they want to take care of. Once you've proven to them you can deliver, you've got a winner.

I was always proud of the work Charlie and I did together, and in 2003, Charlie's agency received our Award of Excellence. His company had issued more than $20 million in premiums for us.

One of the things Union Bankers had done through the years was to bring in motivational speakers, and some of them were huge celebrities. Don Rutherford, who was director of marketing for Union Bankers, was a good friend of Mickey Mantle, and he brought him to five or six conventions. Mickey spoke at two or three of them, and he came to the others just to pal around with us, playing golf and cutting up. He was a funny and very personable guy and a great storyteller, and I got to know him pretty well.

I saw a lot of motivational speakers at conventions through the years, and some were terrific. I was in Kansas City once for a meeting of agents, and Hall of Fame quarterback Len Dawson and I were both on the program. Football players are great because the game translates well to business. You can talk about drive and persistence and second effort and the last-second play that pulls victory from defeat, and it can make an impression. Len gave a great talk, using examples from his career with the Kansas City Chiefs and the big play-off games he'd won.

But I never used motivational speakers at Continental Life. That was my job. The one thing my sister Juanita said would keep me from being a good insurance agent—my speaking ability—turned out to be one of my strong suits. Whether it was one-on-one in somebody's living room, laying out the reasons why she should buy life insurance, in a weekly meeting patting my good salesmen on the back and getting them fired up, or before a crowded ballroom in a fancy hotel laying out a vision and inspiring the people who worked for me, I found that my speaking ability was a real asset. I never thought a sports hero or book author motivated people as much as a leader who was sincerely passionate about the company, its people, and its future. For one thing, they didn't know the company as well. I learned that if you feel it and mean it, your talk will work better than anything you could get from a hired gun.

When it came to speaking, I believed in overpreparing. I would always be ready to cover a lot more ground than I had time for. But then when it came time to speak, I would just talk from my heart. I could key in on what a speaker before me had said or start with something that happened that day, and the rest would just flow. The worst speeches I've ever given were when I wrote everything out and tried to deliver it from the script.

Many people through the years have told me how my enthusiasm and overall leadership rubbed off on them. Many of them who followed my example became very successful, and the thing I'm proudest of is seeing other people progress in the business, seeing them get started with me and watching them grow and develop and become financially independent. I've gotten so many letters over the years from people who have expressed their gratitude and appreciation. My agents and employees knew I cared about them and wanted them to do well. I've been told many times that's why I was so successful—I cared for my people. I always made sure I gave honest and sincere appreciation to everyone who had any part at all in helping the company succeed, from the lady who cleaned the building to the top producer. I thought it was really important to call them by name. That kind of recognition is really the best way—the only way—to make people continue to strive for perfection.

Whenever I spoke at a company gathering, whether it was an awards banquet or a motivational session, I would call out by name someone who had given great service. I'd pick up on little things.

"Sally got out a really important order the other day," I might tell them, singling out someone in supplies. "She got it out because she cared. I couldn't have gone down there and fulfilled that order. I wouldn't be qualified. But Sally was. She knew exactly where to go and what to do to get it done. Sally, that is so important. You are so important. Every cog in this wheel has got to fit. You may not think day in and day out that your job is important, but it is. It's a part of this operation, and this is an important operation. We're doing important things, which means you are doing important things. Without those supplies, that agent could not write that business. Without that business, we wouldn't be able to pay the claims that come in. People wouldn't be able to pay their medical bills. Sally, you're important, and all of you who put your heart into your job are important.

"Success doesn't just happen. It's a matter of people working together for a common cause, to build the finest health insurance company in the industry, rendering the finest service that can be rendered. As a company, we make a promise to the people who buy our policies. I give the people in the home office credit for doing their jobs and doing them well because that's where those promises are fulfilled. That's what helped build the company. These people knock themselves out to see that the promise is fulfilled, properly, efficiently, and with a smile. Each of them has a story to tell about how we delivered a claim or how prompt we were. You're rock solid, and that's the rock I built the company on."

That attitude also kept success from going to my head. Everything contributed to the bottom line. If I saw something lying on the floor, I'd pick it up. If a commode got stopped up, I might go looking for the plunger. Everybody has to be responsible for that sort of thing. It's part of what makes a great company great.

And I never indulged myself in grudges. I can't remember ever hating anybody. I had one executive who had a hard time forgiving people, and I used to talk to him about it. He'd agree that it was counterproductive, that he should do something about it, but he had trouble putting that into practice. I think reading that section in *Think and Grow Rich*—"I will eliminate hatred, envy, jealousy, selfishness, and cynicism"—every day really helped me stay clear of that. It bothers me to see someone else hating or carrying a grudge. It will eat you alive just like cancer. I can always hear my dad saying, "If you can't say something good about somebody, don't say anything at all." That always helped keep me grounded.

So did the lifelong relationships I had with people like my brother Marion and Cecil Ryan. Marion and I were always the closest of our siblings, and Cecil was with me more than forty years, from my early days in the business. There was no putting on airs with them. They knew me underneath the success. Cecil and Marion were my state managers, with Cecil in charge of East Tennessee and Marion, West and Middle Tennessee. They both knew the business inside and out, and they did a great job.

Marion was never jealous. He always respected me, and our relationship was great that way. He was a follower rather than a leader, and he really needed the structure of the company, and so it worked for both of us that we worked together all those years. The one problem I had with him and Cecil was almost laughable. They loved to work together—"two cowboys on one horse," I called it—so they'd sometimes take off in one car together instead of dividing up, like I wanted them to. It was almost like keeping an eye on teenagers. But they were great friends and great employees, honest and dependable. They were a big asset to the company and to me personally.

Marion's son Mike Baskin became a great asset too. He came to work for the company when he was in his mid-twenties, and Marion spent a lot of time with him, giving him the good training that's so important for a new agent coming into the business. He's been a great agent and has always sold business the right way, which is so important. The company has never had complaints from people who've bought policies from him, and he's been a great producer through the years.

I wanted everybody who worked for me to feel appreciated, and there were a lot of ways to go about that. We had a big employee picnic every year. We let them bring their families, and we served them good food and had games to play and prizes they could win. It was a way for them to let their hair down and enjoy each other and our success.

When big agents were in town, I'd take them to the Opry or out to my farm for dinner or for a look at the horses we raised. At conventions, I'd make sure there were goodies in each room. It might be a Tennessee basket with local products or fruit and flowers—things that the agent's wife would appreciate. Making her happy always helped make him happy.

I wanted to be as good to the people who worked for me as I could. Tony Light, my computer and internal operations guy, was going to sell a house and buy another, and I volunteered to go with him as he looked a second time at one he liked. It was decorated really nicely, and I said to the lady who owned it, "This place isn't going to look the same when you take all this pretty stuff out of it." I asked if she could leave one thing and then another, and I finally talked her into leaving behind about $30,000 worth of furniture. Tony absolutely did back flips. He couldn't believe it. He called his wife and told her all about it.

"That big table you liked," he said, "she's leaving it. That cabinet too! The only thing she's going to take is her bedroom furniture."

Then I loaned him the money to buy the house until he sold his own. It took him about a month to sell, and when he did, he paid me back. He couldn't thank me enough. He said, "I told my dad what you were doing and he said, 'People don't do that.'"

I could do things like that because I was doing very well financially. Still, at that point I hadn't been taking much money out of the company. Late in the 1990s I finally upped my salary from $300,000 to $400,000, but my actuary was telling me it was time to do much more.

"You're crazy," he said, "if you don't take more out of here. You need to give yourself two or three million dollars in salary."

My thought was that I owned the company, so the money might as well have been mine. Plus, I always felt like I was building it up, trying to make it bigger, and that meant reinvesting money in it. But he was doing what I paid him to do—keep an eye on the bottom line, and that meant the future as well as the present.

"What if something were to happen?" he said. "Somebody makes a mistake, and all of a sudden you're in the middle of a huge lawsuit. That money might not be there anymore. You're too exposed out there. You need to get some of the money in your own hands."

Finally I did start taking seven-figure salaries, but it took me a couple of years to get them where he wanted.

Chapter 34

My Son Roger Becomes Company President

*Roger became the face of the company
in many ways.*

As I said early on in this book, I often wonder
what might have happened if Jack Schooley had
not called me back when I stood him up that first
day. He got me to believe in myself, to reach for
something I never would have tried otherwise. He
brought me into a business I loved all through my
career, one in which I found more success and
satisfaction than I ever would have dreamed.

As much as Continental Life meant to me, I
knew I couldn't run it forever. I turned sixty-five
in 1997, and although I felt great and was still in
good shape, hitting the traditional retirement age
made me think about the future. I had no desire
to walk away from the business, but I knew I had
to prepare someone to take my place when I did.

If Randy had lived, I believe he would have taken over the company. He was outgoing and wonderful with people. He was a very good salesman and a good executive who had done well in a number of areas of the company. He was a big idea man whose weakness was that he wasn't good at details or follow-through, but you can always hire people to take care of those. His absence as I grew older was another way in which losing him was a blow I never fully overcame.

Roger had done well with the jobs he'd had in the company. He had been claims manager, then administrative vice president, responsible for internal operations, including commission accounting, underwriting, claims, and the supply department. Finally I made him secretary-treasurer.

He had a lot of assets. He got along really well with the employees, and he had overcome a lot of his natural shyness along the way. We'd have meetings with key executives now and then, bringing them in for motivation or to introduce products, and he got to where he was pretty good at getting up and speaking.

Roger had also long ago overcome the habits that had made him a chubby kid. He took health and nutrition very seriously. He worked out regularly and got into great shape. In fact, I used to get on him about taking long lunch breaks so he could sneak in some time in the gym.

He had a great eye for detail, and his interest in the arts and design had really blossomed—he was always involved when we moved to a new place or thought about furnishing a room or house. He was also a "finisher" to a greater extent than Randy had been.

I knew if the company was going to remain a family enterprise, I would have to turn to Roger. He knew the business, he could handle details and follow-through, and the employees liked him. It made sense to let him lead the company while I was active and could guide him. The "sink or swim" part of being the new leader wouldn't be quite so tough that way.

Roger was very comfortable where he was and had shown no interest in becoming president, but it made sense to me to bring him into the position at some point. I knew he'd never had the fire in the belly you need to succeed at the top of a company, but I thought putting him in that position might bring it out of him.

We had big getaways once or twice a year. They were ways of celebrating our success and rewarding our achievers. Often they were in Las Vegas or some other city, but now and then we took a cruise. We had one scheduled in the spring of 1998, and while we were out, the thought of turning over the reins began to consume me. I got caught up in our celebration, and I thought more and more about putting Roger at the helm.

If I'm ever going to do it, I thought, *I just need to go ahead and do it. He'd learn what he had to on the job. I'd be right there.* I made up my mind and I surprised him and everybody else with the announcement that I was making him president. It was a spur-of-the-minute decision, and I think I surprised myself, too.

Roger was thirty-five at the time. He would be chief operating officer as well as president. I would be chairman of the board and chief executive officer. I would oversee the company, with special emphasis on my passion, marketing, and he would run as much of the day-to-day operations as he could. Everybody except my secretary—we had 145 or so employees—would report to him, but I'd always step in to deal with problems.

In reality, I kept doing about what I was doing before. I was still recruiting agents and agencies to sell our products and overseeing most of the business. Whatever my title was, I was going to do anything that needed to be done.

We did very well in the years after he became president. We kept growing like crazy. In 2002, we processed 25 percent more applications than in 2001. In 2003, the figure jumped another 24 percent. Cash premium receipts rose from $104 to $128 million from 2002 to 2003.

Roger became the face of the company in many ways. He gave out awards and pressed the flesh when he had to, although that was never something he was completely comfortable with. He told me he envied my ability to get up in front of a group of friends or strangers and speak from the heart and really grab them.

For a while, I was excited about the transition. I pictured generations of Baskins running the company. Roger did well at a lot of the tasks that go into running a company, but it wasn't long before I knew I knew it wasn't something that was destined to work. There's a lot of psychology I could put into analyzing it, but the bottom line is, I'd given Roger something he didn't want, something he'd never asked for and wasn't ready for. You don't learn fire in the belly. It's there or it isn't. Roger hadn't earned the position. It was just handed to him. He would have been content to stay where he was. He didn't put the hours or the energy into the position that I did, and that caused friction between us.

Part of it was generational. Roger was from a different era than me or even Randy. Randy had grown up at a time when Sadie and I didn't have much of anything. Roger came along when things were good, and that makes a difference. I was a workaholic—still am—and he was more laid-back about business. I tried to lead by example, and then I tried to talk him into taking more of my approach, but it just wasn't him. Being president of a company that size is a high-pressure occupation, and Roger wasn't cut out for it. I saw him lose interest, and finally he told me he wanted to leave the company, to go into business for himself. He got his general contractor's license and started building high-dollar homes, and I took over again as president. I think it was a big relief to him.

I had wanted the company to stay in the family. Now I could see that wasn't going to happen. It had never occurred to me to sell it, even though I could have earned a lot of money doing so. Now at last the thought crossed my mind.

Chapter 35

Regulation Changes The Business

*In 2003, President Bush
signed into law the biggest
Medicare change ever,
adding prescription drugs
to the list of covered charges.*

The insurance business of the 2000s was radically different from the one I entered in the 1950s. The first and most profound change came during the presidency of Lyndon Johnson. The medical profession had fought for decades to keep health insurance private, saying government involvement would interfere with the doctor-patient relationship and hurt physicians' income. They fought particularly hard against the 1943 Wagner-Murray-Dingell Bill, which would have provided nationalized health insurance to all Americans. Proponents of nationalized health insurance then began focusing on the elderly and the poor, and that led to the 1965 creation of Medicare and Medicaid. From that point on, Medicare supplement policies became a key offering of private insurers, and they provided much of the focus of my career. Through the years it wasn't hard to demonstrate to people that they needed a policy that filled in the gaps in what Medicare covered. I used to put together full-page looks at the progression of co-payments and deductibles, both of which increased nineteen times in twenty years. I'd send them to our policyholders and run them in the newsletter for our agents, reminding them of the importance of coverage that kept up with those changes, as ours was designed to do.

Federal and state governments gradually exerted more control over the business, getting ever more involved in the day-to-day dealings of insurance companies. It became a huge concern. State insurance departments controlled rate increases, dictating the way companies were paid. They required more premium dollars to go back to the consumer in the form of claims payments, causing claims losses to be higher than the companies wanted them, which is why companies don't make any profit selling insurance. They earn their money on investment income.

At one point, the National Association of Insurance Commissioners, a nonprofit organization founded in 1971 to coordinate state regulations, wanted states to adopt a 65 percent claims ratio as standard. That would have had a serious impact on an agent's net income.

Over the years, the feds changed the commission structure, and that was one instance where government intrusion actually helped deal with a real problem. When companies were giving big commissions up front—the kind that could let me earn 70 percent of the first year's premium in some cases—some agents were tempted to roll business, canceling a policy a year or two down the road and writing a new one for the customer and then collecting that big commission again. The feds made companies spread the commission over several years, which took the incentive out of rolling policies.

In other areas, yes, there were companies that were taking advantage of the system, just like there were agents doing that, but the cure was usually worse than the disease. Some of the rules made no economic sense. To take just one example, Arkansas mandated that everyone who took out Medicare supplement insurance pay the same premium, whether you were sixty-five or eighty-five. What that means, of course, is that you're overcharging the relatively healthier sixty-five-year-olds and undercharging the less-healthy eighty-five-year-olds.

There was another one I hated. When a company went bankrupt, the state would step in and take it over, collecting money from the other companies doing business there to pay the outstanding claims. That meant that when some company that had been giving me fits for years went broke, I'd have to help pay their claims in a formula based on our premium income—the bigger your company, the more you'd have to pay to offset another company's losses. I'd see a company go under, and not long afterward I'd get a bill in the mail from the state. It used to gall me to no end.

As the population aged and became more affluent, there were more prospects and more money out there, but there were far more challenges. The government dictated how a company could approach potential clients. You couldn't knock on doors anymore, and the no-call list took millions of people out of phone reach. You were supposed to mail out solicitations and get cards or phone calls back to open the door. Under the new rules, prospecting was very difficult.

We had to get better at finding and contacting potential clients. We subscribed to a company that furnished us with a list of callable names they would update every so often. I'd have people in the office calling and saying, "We're going to have a representative in your area tomorrow. May he stop by to show you how you can protect yourself when it comes to the new changes in Medicare?" We'd get a 2 or 3 percent response that way. I remember once a guy in Mississippi was getting 6 or 7 percent response, and I made sure I mentioned that in the newsletter. Any time an agent did something spectacular, I wrote about it. It was a chance to reward him, give other agents hints on how to be better salesmen, and keep them hungry and competitive, all at the same time.

That happened with leads. An agent had to pay six bucks or so for a good lead, and he was supposed to turn it into an application or send it back as no good. A good agent would go back and work a no-good lead. He'd call and say, "We're just doing a follow-up. We sent a young man out there to make a sales call and just wanted to make sure he actually called on you." Once he had them talking, he'd ask what the person thought about the salesman and the policy, and a good agent could turn that no into another sales call and a buy.

There were a couple of legislative scares in the 1980s. Congress at one point threatened to repeal the 1945 McCarran-Ferguson Act, which exempted the insurance business from most federal regulations, including some antitrust laws. It would have strengthened the hand of the federal government tremendously in controlling the industry. Such a bill passed the House in 2012 but had not been voted on in the Senate by July 2012.

There was a big scare in 1988 with the Medicare Catastrophic Coverage Act, which expanded Medicare benefits to include outpatient drugs and capped co-payment for other services. It was the biggest expansion of Medicare since its inception, and it scared the insurance industry. Many in the industry lobbied against it. Senior citizens objected to the new taxes and the likelihood that their insurance premiums would go up, and they put enough pressure on Congress that it was quickly repealed.

In 2003, President Bush signed into law the biggest Medicare change ever, adding prescription drugs to the list of covered charges. It wasn't something that affected us much on a business level. Its only real effect on us as a company was that it gave agents something to talk about with prospective clients. It was a door opener.

The state and federal changes came incrementally, and none of them made life easier for the insurance industry. When government gets involved, it's generally not good. But that becomes the new reality, and you have to accept it. You just work with whatever conditions the government imposes on business.

I can honestly say, though, that if I'd known in the old days how complex the insurance industry was going to become, how strict and bothersome the regulations were going to be, I don't know that I would have gotten into it. I know I would have done a lot more thinking about it. So often you're dealing with a neophyte in a government bureau who really doesn't understand what's going on, but he's got a set of rules he's got to enforce. It's just a tough row to hoe.

Then there were the business changes. The industry itself was constantly in flux, with companies adding and tweaking products, looking for the combination of premiums and benefits that would give them an edge with the average buyer, and all the time competing with you not only for customers but also for the best agents.

There were also outside entities. Nothing hit bigger than the HMO's. The Health Maintenance Organization Act of 1973 mandated that firms with twenty-five or more employees had to offer an HMO option. An HMO provides health coverage with "gatekeepers" who okay or deny coverage beyond doctor visits, placing an emphasis on preventive care. The premiums are generally lower than for standard insurance coverage, but restrictions on service and a loss of control over which health care professionals a consumer can see often led to customer dissatisfaction.

The federal government contracted with HMO's to provide what amounted to federally subsidized Medicare supplement policies, which put them in direct competition with us. It got especially bad in the last years I ran the company. In fact, it caused us more problems than anything I'd encountered in my years in the business. A Medicare recipient wouldn't have to pay a dime to get HMO-based supplemental coverage. It's hard to compete with free, and we lost a lot of business in those years.

The trick was that the restrictions on service and the fact that people were told which doctors and hospitals to use made a lot of people very unhappy. They'd face denial of treatment or tests they thought they needed in life-and-death situations. They'd be unable to go to a doctor they'd had for years. In fact, we used to run "HMO Horror Stories" in our newsletter. People gradually saw that it was worth what an insurance company charged to be able to have more control when it came to choosing doctors and services. Many of them, after a year or two and a couple of bad experiences, came back to us. But that was a mixed blessing. Many times people came back after, say, contracting cancer and having trouble getting good treatment. Federal law said we had to take them back again with no additional underwriting, which meant we took a huge hit. I never thought that was fair either.

As a company gets older, there are other economic changes. Early in the life of a policy or a company, you're earning a lot of money on premiums, and you're not paying out much in the way of claims. That changes through the years. Your policyholders get older, and their health worsens. That's especially true when most of what you do is Medicare supplement policies, as it was for us. You can't be afraid of claims if you're going to get into the Medicare supplement business because you're going to get a lot of them. By the mid-2000s, I was paying out $100,000 a day in claims—more than $1 million every two weeks. You've got to bring in new policyholders to replace your aging ones, which gets tougher because you've got to keep raising your rates to make up for the increased claims. That was true even with my strict underwriting, although it was less of a burden to me than it was to my competition. Most of the time my rate increases were half of my competition's. If they asked for 20 percent, I'd be asking for 10, or maybe 12, even late in my career.

For many years, an insurance company could deal with aging policyholders and rising premiums simply by issuing another, similar policy and selling it to a new pool of people. It would be essentially like starting over. The government stopped that, so the only way to do that afterward was to start a completely new company. That's exactly what I did in 2005 when I started American Continental Insurance Company, which offered a Medicare supplement at a lower premium than we could offer through Continental.

By about that time, though, I was thinking about retirement. I turned seventy in 2002. I still loved the business, but I knew I didn't want to maintain the pace I'd kept up for all those years. I always believed in keeping weekends for family, and I believed in getting away and enjoying life. It was time for me to do more of that, to enjoy our horses and our Prevost motor coach. The increasing challenges in dealing with the government and HMO's made it an easier decision. Then, once Roger decided he didn't want to lead the company, the thought of selling made sense. I didn't like it, but it was the only practical thing to do. Nobody else was really in a position to run the company for us. If I could have come up with another option, I would have, but the time had come.

I started dealing with a California firm that screened potential buyers, and that led me to Genworth Financial, one of the largest life insurance companies in the country. Having a firm that size interested in the company I founded and built was a real honor. It was pretty high cotton for a Tennessee hillbilly who didn't have any more sense than to go out there and work.

We talked for months, and I sent them stacks and stacks of documents so they could see on paper what they knew by reputation—that this was a company worth buying. We were well on the road to a deal at the time of the CLI convention in the spring of 2005. I had delivered a speech to a group of agents, and afterward I was sitting by the hotel pool with a group that included my grandson Rafe. His real name is Randall Baskin III, and he is Randy's oldest. He'd been born about the time I started the company, and he was twenty-three. Rafe had worked for a few years in the home office, recruiting agents on the phone, and then he'd gone out into the field, where he'd done pretty well as a salesman. He'd actually won the trip to Vegas, selling enough insurance to qualify. He had seen my speech, and he was going on and on about how impressed he was.

"Granddad," he said, "I'm so proud of you. I watched the crowd while you were speaking. You had those people eating out of your hand. It's amazing how you can capture an audience. And people flocked around you afterward to talk to you. You've got a lot of people that really believe in you and Continental."

I think he saw the power of an idea, of motivation, of leadership, and got carried away with wanting to be a part of that. He said that it would be heartbreaking to see the company pass into someone else's hands and that he wanted me to keep it in the family. He was willing to do whatever it took to help. I could groom him to be my replacement over the next couple of years.

"Will you think about it?" he said.

He was pretty persuasive. I thought about it and decided he was right. I shouldn't sell. Looking back, I can see he was saying just what I wanted to hear. I had put my life into the company for a long time, and I wanted to see it stay in the family. Randy was gone, and Roger had decided the business wasn't for him. Rafe, in one of the best bits of salesmanship he'd ever done, sold me on keeping the company.

When we got back home, I talked to my lawyer and my internal operations man, Tony Light, and told them I'd decided to call off the deal.

"So, you're sure about this?" they said. They were pretty shocked.

I told them about Rafe and our conversation and said that I'd made up my mind. We drafted a letter and sent it to the company.

"Okay," Genworth said, "if that's what you want. We'll go ahead and destroy all the paperwork you sent us."

Then there were our own people to deal with. The word had gotten around that we were talking about selling. I knew that for the sake of morale I had to put a stop to the rumors. I used a full page in the next issue of the newsletter to address the rumors and ended by saying, "This company is not for sale."

I was pretty happy for a while. Rafe was eventually going to take over. I was sure that he was out there on fire for the company, selling up a storm, and that before long I'd bring him in and start showing him the ropes.

The trouble was, he wasn't showing up among the sales leaders anymore. And then I stopped hearing from him.

I realized pretty quickly that I'd made a mistake.

Rafe simply didn't follow through on his promise. He was very young, and I think his enthusiasm was paper thin and didn't hold up when he looked at the reality of it. He had been talking the talk, but he wasn't walking the walk.

On my way home one day, pretty annoyed with him, I called him on my cell phone. The call went to his voice mail. I knew he could see my number and just didn't want to talk. I happened to have another phone in the car, so I called him on that one. He didn't know it was me, and he picked up. At that point I let him have it. I chewed him out until I was almost ashamed of myself.

The next morning I went into my attorney's office and met with him and my director of internal affairs. I told them I wanted to sell again.

"You're going to have to see if they're still interested," my attorney said.

"Well," I told him, "get them on the phone."

They were still interested. Now, though, since they had destroyed all those documents, we had to go back and re-create a stack of paper three feet high. It probably cost me $10,000 or $15,000 just to reproduce it.

What's more, now Genworth was skeptical. They thought something might have happened that had affected the value or outlook of the company. I didn't blame them. I was kicking my tail for cutting off the sale. I was lucky they were still interested, since a company our size doesn't normally fool around like that.

They looked at everything again and satisfied themselves that we weren't trying to pull anything underhanded. Finally we closed the deal. My business career had come to a close.

Chapter 36

Selling The Company

"You know the seventy-five cents you used to give me and Brother every Monday morning?" I said. "It's been drawing interest all these years."

When I sold the company, I had 146 people in the home office. Genworth immediately hired 15 more. It was one of many things I didn't understand about the way they handled Continental Life, but it wasn't mine anymore and so there was nothing I could say.

For the first six months after the sale, I really wished I hadn't sold it. It took me about a year to start getting used to the fact that I no longer owned it. It took much longer to start feeling that it was the right thing to do. Then in 2008, the economy went into a tailspin, and I began to realize I had definitely sold the company at the right time. By 2010 it probably would have brought $50 million less than what I sold it for, which was $145 million. The timing actually couldn't have been better.

I invested the sale price, and Tony, my operations guy, asked what kind of interest I was able to get. I told him I was getting 5.5 percent. He did some quick figuring and told me I would be earning $18,000 per day on that money. I added some other cash I had to that investment and took into account what Genworth was paying me in rent for the office building, and it turned out I was earning $1,000 an hour, twenty-four hours a day, 365 days a year.

I was pretty excited until Tony and I realized we had failed to consider the taxes. My tax bill for the year 2006 was $22,810,516. I called my CPA, Don Coomer, and had him run the numbers for 2007, after the taxes had been paid. It came to $22,050 a day, or $919 per hour. Given where I had started in life, it was almost more than I could comprehend. And it sure wasn't a bad retirement income.

I do miss working to some extent. I was driven to build my career, the agency, and then the company, and they had consumed my life for all those years. But I keep busy now. Sadie and I spend time traveling and working with the horses. I enjoy reading more than ever, and my first choice is still inspirational. I love Rhonda Byrnes's *The Secret* and the follow-up, *The Power*, which I've read half a dozen times now.

I keep an eye on my investments, which is no easy task in an economy like this one. I also keep an eye out for good things I can do with the money.

Roger was relieved that he didn't have to stay with the company, although I think he had second thoughts after the housing bubble burst and business became a real struggle.

Rafe went through a period where his sales just weren't what I thought they should be, but everything changed when his stepdad, a developer, spotted and developed a piece of property not far from where I live. He knew there was a road coming through that would make the entire thing more valuable, and Rafe wanted one of the lots so he could build a rental house. At the same time, he found another house he wanted to live in. He came to me and asked me to help him, and I loaned him the money for both. From that point on, he's been right on top of things. He hasn't been late on a single payment, and he's been working as hard as I could have hoped.

Rafe is a born salesman, someone who can draw people in with the force of his personality. He'll call me from the road and tell me about something he's just sold and say, "Granddad, I'm a baa-a-a-ad man." Then he'll tell me what he's sold. He's been studying my career, even reading the inspirational books I've read, borrowing my copies so he can see exactly what I've underlined, trying to learn from my example. He also uses my success to his advantage, talking about our relationship if a prospect knows me or mentions one of the institutions I'm involved with. He goes to church every Sunday morning with Sadie and me, and I was so happy when he joined not long ago. Looking back on the days when he wanted me to keep the company in the family, I have to say he was just too young. If he'd been just a little older, the business might well still be in the family. Since then, he's really come into his own, and he's making me very proud.

I was at a condo we owned in Clearwater, Florida, in October 2004 when our internal operations guy and old friend Tony Light called and told me Marion had a heart attack. Marion was my brother and my best friend. We were always close, working together, traveling, and taking vacations together with Sadie and Dot, and he would do anything for me.

"How is he?" I said.

"He's dead."

He was that blunt. I almost fell over. It was the biggest shock I'd received since Randy's accident, and I still miss him a great deal.

The last of my siblings to die was Betty, and there's no overstating the importance she had in my life. The unselfishness she showed as a teenage girl is with me to this day. She showed me that any of us, no matter how little we have or how little we earn, can make a huge difference to others if we're willing to think beyond ourselves. I don't know that she ever really knew how much the seventy-five cents she gave to me and to Marion so we could buy lunch at school meant to me.

In May of 2004, just a few years before she died, she and I were at a Tennessee Walking Horse event together.

"Betty," I said, "I want you to do something for me."

"What's that?"

"When we get home, I want you to go pick out a new car. Whatever you want. I want to buy you one."

She looked at me funny. "Why are you going to buy me a new car?" she asked.

"You know the seventy-five cents you used to give me and Brother every Monday morning?" I said. "It's been drawing interest all these years, and I just want to buy you a new car."

She'd always liked Buicks, and I thought she'd buy something really fancy, but she didn't. She called a few days later and said she'd picked out a Buick SUV. It cost about $35,000, and we went down together and I bought it for her.

This is the letter I gave her at the time...

Dear Betty:

The experiences that impact us the most are those we seem to carry with us for a lifetime. As a poor, young boy growing up in Murfreesboro, I could not have imagined the prosperity that lay outside the walls of our old homeplace. Today as I look back, I can hardly imagine being so poor.

I have recounted a thousand times the story of our struggles growing up, how you gave so much at a time when we had so little and how you worked so unselfishly to see that Marion and I had the $1.50 we needed weekly for lunch money. Each time I recall the sacrifices you made, it's as if I am remembering it for the first time. The unselfish examples you set of hard work and perseverance I have carried with me to this day.

It is with great joy that I am able to present you this new Buick, in appreciation for all you have done for me. It hardly compares to the sacrifices you have made for Marion and me. Please accept it with all the gratitude I feel.

With affection
Randall

It turned out to be the first brand-new car she'd ever owned, and I wouldn't take anything for the opportunity I had to buy it for her. She taught me lessons about hard work, about family, and about helping others that have stayed with me all of my life, and that's something for which I'm very, very grateful.

PART IV
LOVING LIFE

Chapter 37

Wealth As A Blessing

*You set your mind working toward
that goal, and then all of a sudden
you realize, I could have this.*

Success has given me many things. I have
friends all over the country. I have had the
opportunity many times to make a difference
in other people's lives, sometimes by example,
sometimes with the things I say, and sometimes
with charitable giving.

This is an age when many people mistrust
those who have money. Whatever opinion you
might have on the matter, I want to talk about the
effect that money has had on my life. I've talked
about where I came from. I know what it is to be
poor. And I've talked about where my journey led.
I know what it is to be rich.

Having wealth has allowed Sadie and me
to do many things we could never have done
otherwise, but it hasn't fundamentally changed
us or the things we enjoy. I don't know anyone

who feels uncomfortable around us. I get a lot of compliments on the fact that I have not let success go to my head, that I don't put on the dog. People say I'm still the Randall Baskin I was when I had nothing. I feel proud that I've kept the friends I had when I was poor alongside the friends I've made on the high side. I've seen a lot of people get money or authority, and if neither one goes to his head, I consider him a pretty level-headed guy. I hope that description fits me.

Sadie is even more down to earth than I am. Our house is big and beautiful, but Sadie would have been content in the one that was here when we bought the property. We do have a maid, but I've been known to clean the windows when she hasn't gotten to them, and I'm not afraid to do anything else that needs doing. We drive nice automobiles, but it's not about showing off. We also have a Prevost motor coach with all the conveniences of home, but that's just the latest chapter in a love of travel that goes back to when we were first married.

Eventually we got out of the motor homes and bought a condo on the beach in Clearwater, and later a second one in Panama City. Then we started buying the Prevosts. I've often laughed about the fact that there were two things I said I wouldn't be when I was young—an insurance man and a truck driver. It turned out I spent my life in the insurance business and used part of the money to buy and drive the next best thing to a truck—a big bus.

Our Florida trips gradually became a combination of fun and business. I'd do the real work in a morning meeting, and then sometimes I'd meet someone for lunch. The people whose company I really enjoyed—like Larry Franklin, who was always great to be around—I'd take to dinner.

I traveled a lot during those years and got to spend a lot of time with friends and family—Marion and Dot went with us on a lot of those trips, and Randy went on quite a few. Those times were special, and life was good. In fact, I always made it a point to enjoy life. I often turned our convention trips into vacations, leaving afterward for a few days somewhere warm. On two occasions when Union Bankers held its convention in Las Vegas, Sadie and I and Don Rutherford, who was director of marketing for the company, and his wife, Linda, flew on out to San Diego and spent four or five days there. There were great conventions in Phoenix, too, and some unforgettable times at the Princess Hotel in Acapulco. Don was a great promotion man who could take you to what was happening in just about any city. He would set up our Acapulco stays and rent a home for us in an elegant part of the city overlooking Acapulco Bay, next door to the house where Henry Kissinger spent his honeymoon. When I saw the view from that balcony for the first time, watching the city's lights twinkle like stars with the moon shining on the bay, I realized why Acapulco was known as the most romantic place in the world. It's the most beautiful place I could imagine, and it was elegant—every morning the people who took care of the house would cook whatever we had requested the day before. A group of us—Don and Linda, Marion and Dot, Joe and Marian White—went there for three years straight in the mid-1980s.

Sadie and I also took a vacation to Hawaii and liked it enough to go back six more times. The only drawback is the jet lag—it takes you a day or two to get feeling good because your sleeping gets all messed up. The last time we went I told Sadie, "I think I'll let that be my last trip," and it was.

Closer to home, our getaway in Giles County was something we treasured for many years. It was a beautiful place out in the country, and Marion and I worked our tails off cutting trails through the woods and clearing off a spot where we built a cabin. Marion and Dot and Sadie and I and our friend Jack Featherstone and his wife, Doris, who had the place across the street, would go out there every weekend. I remember wonderful winter nights when we'd build a fire and talk and laugh, telling jokes and stories until all hours. We'd ride our horses and four-wheelers through the woods, and Marion and I would go squirrel hunting. We had a lot of great times out there, but we sold it after Randy's accident.

Home has always been important to us, going back to the days when we so desperately wanted a home of our own, even if the roof leaked and there was no running water. For years we lived in a big house we built on Old Hickory Boulevard in Brentwood, but we always kept our eye on a big farm just south of Franklin. We used to see it from I-65 every time we drove by. We loved that farm and the rolling hills it sat on, and I could just picture us living there. At one point it came on the market, and we inquired about it. It had ninety-five acres and a nice rock house, and the asking price was $3 million—which at that time was way out of reach for us.

But we kept dreaming. It was what I did with everything. Achieving goals begins with envisioning them. You imagine the things you want to attain. At first they may be there only in dim outline, but you keep working and achieving and they get a little clearer. In the old days, when I first saw the numbers the regional manager for Union Bankers in Mississippi was earning, I just couldn't believe it. Even when I realized the company wasn't lying to me, the thought of earning that much money was a hazy one. Then as I passed one and then another of the agents between me and him, that thought became a vision that kept getting clearer and more real.

You set your mind to working toward that goal, and then all of a sudden you realize, I could have this. I could achieve it. It gets to where you think, *It's as good as mine.* That's the way things happen, and that's the way it was with this farm.

Mr. Cross, who bought the place when it came on the market, was a successful real estate developer who was also in the horse business. He owned it for several years and then got very ill. Not long after he died—it was shortly after Randy was killed—a friend in the real estate business came to me.

"You know," she said, "the Cross farm you like so much is for sale." First American Bank had taken it over. It was one of many properties they had, and they just wanted to be rid of it. The place had gone into disrepair during the year and a half Mr. Cross was sick, and the bank was asking just $475,000. There was another offer on the table for $450,000, but they were looking for the full price. I took my Prevost out and spent two nights there to see if the noise from nearby I-65 would bother me. It didn't. Still, I hesitated.

My attorney said, "Randall, what does twenty-five thousand dollars mean to you?"

"What do you mean?"

"You know twenty-five thousand dollars is nothing to you. You've already told me it's a steal. If I wanted that place, I'd pay what they're asking. If you offer anything less, you're giving that other guy the chance to come in and beat you to it."

To this day, I always say I need to hug his neck. I paid what they were asking and bought it right out from under the other bidder. My years with Sadie in that place have been almost too good to be true.

We lived in the rock house for two years while we built the big house I wanted. I wanted some of me in every place we lived, and this was going to be the big expression of my personality and a celebration of success. Roger moved into the white house at the front of the property and Sadie and I moved into the stone house while we built the big house. I had a backhoe that I used on the farm we had in Giles County and another on McDaniel Road, and I had gotten really good with it. I had practiced in Giles County. I'd go into the woods and find a spot and start working the levers, seeing what each one did. I got to where I could dig a pretty good hole, and then I'd cover it back up and start again. Eventually I got to where I'd tell people, "I could pick your teeth with it."

Not many people have ever planned a house as thoroughly as I planned that one. I'd go to the spot where I wanted the house and I'd sit in the backhoe, then stand up and say, "That's the view I want from the porch. This is the height it needs to be."

The way the ground was, we had to pour the foundation pretty deep and put steel in it. The bottom of the basement was going to be sitting six feet in the air. That meant I had to bring in a lot of dirt, and I do mean a lot. I had a bulldozer operator push a lot of dirt into a big pile at one spot on the property and then I went to work. I'd get the backhoe and load up a dump truck, then haul that dirt to the house and dump it next to the foundation. Then I'd take the backhoe and level it out and then go back and fill the dump truck again. When that pile of dirt was gone, I'd have the bulldozer push up another pile. I made hundreds of trips back and forth, up and down the hill, weekend after weekend. Where the driveway led to the garage, I had to fill in with gravel, and there's no telling how many loads I brought in. Eventually I got it built up to where I could bring in asphalt and make the driveway.

The water lines were going to run from the road to both houses, and I dug the ditches and put in the lines. Then I put in the drain lines taking the water away from the downspouts around the house, planning it so that the water ran down into the lake. I also ran a line from the river, a thousand feet away, to water the yard.

All that work had the same basic shape as any of the work I've done. I held in my mind the vision of that house, and when all the dirt was packed around it and the water lines were in and the house was completed and then furnished, I could see it as an expression of the dream I had as a boy and the determination it planted in me. I could see success as something tangible, something real, something I could walk through and enjoy.

It's got nine thousand square feet, with an unfinished third floor that would make it fourteen thousand. It's got five bedrooms, each with its own balcony, six full baths and three half-baths, four fireplaces and four porches, and a six-car garage with four doors. It's got a large second-floor office that overlooks the living room, a media room with its own kitchen, and a recreation room with a large balcony overlooking the pool, fountains, and lake. There's also a nice barn, a big equipment shed, and a nice little house by the gate.

I bring friends and business associates to the place and walk them through the barns and show them the horses, then show them the buffalo out in the front pasture. And when Sadie and I look out from the back porch between its columns at the pool, the lake, and the fountain, or have breakfast on the cozy side porch, I can't tell you how good it feels. And sure enough, the elevation is just right.

After our early years in my parents' house, her parents' house, and that leaky old trailer, it's still sometimes hard to believe we live somewhere this nice, but we do and we take our full measure of enjoyment from it. And for me it will always be an example of the power of constructive dreaming.

Chapter 38

The Walking Horse Business

Sure enough, Out on Parole went in and won the World Grand Championship.

Back in 1988, my wife and younger son, Roger, bought a Tennessee Walking Horse named Pushin' and Shovin'. Sadie had grown up around horses, like I had, and she got to missing them. I don't think she or Roger had a clue what they were getting into, and I didn't know a thing about Walking Horses. Roger started showing the horse at events around Middle Tennessee, and I'd tag along just out of curiosity. I had no idea what made a good or bad Walking Horse, so I didn't really know what I was looking for. I watched and hoped that Pushin' and Shovin' would win, but he never did. Sadie and Roger realized pretty quickly that they had a thing or two to learn about the sport.

I had no way of knowing it at the time, but that purchase was the start of a love affair with Tennessee Walking Horses that I've been part of ever since. My interest started slowly. I began meeting people involved in the sport, and I got to asking questions and picking up a little information here and there. I gradually learned how you judge a good horse by the way it holds its head, by the straight line it maintains up through the shoulder, by the easy way it takes those long strides without looking cramped.

Once I learned a little, it occurred to me that if you're going to be in the horse business, you might as well buy something that's going to win some shows. I bought some horses here and there, and once in a while we'd mess up and win a ribbon. For a long time, any ribbon of any color was a thrill to us. Then in the late 1990s, I paid $125,000 for a horse named Juke Walken, and I knew we really had something. In 1998, he was 15.2-hands-and-under Grand Champion. That was our first big win.

All of us kept learning, and finally in April of 2002, Roger called me and said he'd found a great horse, an up-and-coming two-year-old named Out on Parole. The owner wanted $40,000 for him. Our trainer, Steve Dunn, one of the best in the business, told me, "If you're going to buy him, you'd better buy him now. They don't know what they have." I agreed to the price sight unseen. I learned later that Bob Kilgore, who's big in the Walking Horse business, bought the horse out of the field as a weanling. His wife told him he shouldn't sell the horse because of the way he held his head—how proud he looked as he walked—but Mr. Kilgore sold him to a Mr. Hammonds for $16,000. Not long afterward, Mr. Hammonds had open-heart surgery and decided to get out of the business. Part of their deal gave Mr. Kilgore the right of first refusal if Mr. Hammonds decided to sell the horse, so Mr. Hammonds called and said, "I've got an offer from Randall Baskin on this horse at $40,000. Do you want him back at that price?" Mr. Kilgore told him to go ahead and sell.

"It's the worst mistake I made in the horse business," Mr. Kilgore said later.

Six months later, we took Out on Parole to the Tennessee Walking Horse National Celebration, an eleven-day event held annually in Shelbyville, Tennessee, through the Saturday night before Labor Day. Before we ever put him in the big arena to compete, Mr. Kilgore took another look at him, realized what he'd let slip away, and offered me $250,000 for him. That horse just walked proud, his head high with an almost perfect shake, stepping high with a long reach and a long stride in his rear. It was like he was saying, "Just look at me. I know I'm good." Bob Cherry, one of the legends among Tennessee Walking Horse breeders, came and told me, "I've been at this game for thirty years. You've got the best horse that I've ever seen. He's going to win the big one."

Sure enough, Out on Parole—by then we were calling him OOPS for short—went in and won the World Championship. The next week, on August 31, he won the World Grand Championship. The feeling afterward was a high I had never experienced. Everyone was congratulating me and patting me on the back. Reporters crowded around me, wanting to get the story. Over the next few days and weeks, stories appeared everywhere. I've still got a scrapbook filled with articles from various newspapers.

After the win, Bob came up to me and said, "What did I tell you?" At that point, Mr. Kilgore offered me $750,000 and I probably could have gotten $1 million, but OOPS wasn't for sale.

As a three-year-old, OOPS won the World Championship and lost the World Grand Championship, the only loss he ever had in the big arena. He won both championships as a four-year-old and as a five-year-old.

I've had literally dozens of old-timers tell me that my horse will go down in history as being one of the four or five all-time great Tennessee Walking Horses, and he's proven it to me over and over. Today he is one of the nation's leading breeding stallions. During the 2011 Celebration, he was the sire of sixteen blue ribbon winners, six reserve World Grand Champions, and twenty-two other Celebration winners. He has become known as the stallion that puts winners in the show ring! The 2011 edition of *The Year in Walking Horses*, published by The Walking Horse Report, was dedicated to OOPS to acknowledge all he has done for the breed.

OOPS is also one of the sweetest horses I've ever run across. He doesn't have a mean bone in his body. He's very smart, and he loves attention. If a little child comes up to put his halter on, he'll hold his head way down low for that child.

One of his offspring, Folsom Prison Blues, has won a number of championships, and another may be even better. I bought Mister Heisman as a three-year-old, and soon afterward he became three-year-old World Champion. Watching him win the state class in Tunica, Mississippi, was the biggest thrill I've had since Out on Parole won the big one. Our friends were just as thrilled for us. After that win, I told Sadie that most people in the business go a lifetime without ever being fortunate enough to have one great horse, and it looks like we're going to have two.

Unfortunately, the Walking Horse business is not what it once was. The downturn in the economy hit it especially hard, and so many people were breeding horses during the boom years that the prices came way down. Allegations of soring, an illegal practice in which horses are injured by chemical and other means to make them step higher, and government investigations into them are hurting the industry as well.

I still love the business, and I'm hopeful about it. My office has paintings and photos of OOPS to remind me of our success, and I still have trainers working with many of the offspring of OOPS and various brood mares. I have a dozen or so horses in training, and Sadie and I spend every Thursday with the horses and trainers. We still take our Prevost to Shelbyville every year for the championship. I want to see the business come back strong, and I believe it will.

Chapter 39

Time:
The Great Equalizer

*The people who succeed
are those who maintain
a positive attitude
and keep their sights on their goals.*

Time is the world's most precious commodity, and it increases in value every day. "Do not squander time," Ben Franklin said, "for time is the stuff life is made of."

The first twenty years of a person's life move slowly. Summers seem to stretch out indefinitely. A school year can last forever. Once you get into the real world, time seems to speed up. We are here for a short while, and the older you get, the more you realize just how precious time is. The secret to success is how you use that time.

Early in my career, I ran across this poem and quoted it aloud often. In fact, I was so impressed with it at one time I had it printed on the back of my business card. The author is unknown.

TODAY
This is the beginning of a new day. God
has given me this day to use as I will. I
can waste it or use it for good. What I do is
important because I am exchanging a day
of my life for it. When tomorrow comes, this
day will be gone forever, leaving in its place
something I've traded for it. I want to win,
not lose; I want good, not evil;
I want success, not failure, in order that I
won't regret the price I paid for it.

I see young people coming out of college who
can't make up their minds about what they want
to do. I see them killing another day, another
week, another month, and it really bothers me to
see them wasting time.

Yes, the economic landscape is different, but even
in a bad economy there are opportunities. It may
take more work to find them, but they're available;
people started careers and earned fortunes even
during the darkest days of the Depression.

I had no choice when it came to working. I had
to keep Sadie and Randy and me fed. Fortunately,
I knew how to work hard, and that habit served
me well. One of the problems many young people
have is affluence or, at least, comfort. So many of
them have never faced real want. Growing up poor
was one of the key ingredients in my success. I
think it always kept me at least a little bit hungry.
Country singer Ronnie Dunn said it probably as
well as anyone: "I don't care how much money I
have. I will always be poor because I have that
poor man's mentality I was born with." That
describes me too.

I've talked throughout this book about Jack Schooley and Earl Nightingale and Napoleon Hill and the others whose inspiration served me so well through the years. I should add that I'm convinced that the place of my birth was the foundation upon which all of my success was built. Being born in America is probably the greatest asset a child could ask for. This is truly the land of opportunity, where you're still limited only by the size of your dreams and your willingness to work. We still produce Bill Gates and Steve Jobs and countless other innovators and entrepreneurs who take good ideas and hard work and earn fortunes while they make life better and more convenient for all of us. Part of the reason for this book is to remind people that those days are not over. Innovation and hard work have not gone out of style, and they still produce wonderful results today.

The best way to keep your mind positive is through goal setting. The people who succeed are those who maintain a positive attitude and keep their sights on their goals. When that approach becomes a way of life and it's backed up by hard work and good ideas, success flows as naturally as water.

We are the sum total of our thoughts. Both poverty and riches are the offspring of thought, for thought is the seed of our destinies. Today's decisions are tomorrow's reality.

We are at this moment where our thoughts of yesteryear and yesterday have brought us, and our thoughts of today will determine where we will be and what we will be doing in the tomorrows to come. I think this is where the motivational books and the Bible, the ultimate motivational book, agree. Man follows the thoughts that he holds in his mind: "Be careful what you think, because your thoughts run your life" (Proverbs 4:23 NEW CENTURY VERSION). Therefore, the secret of success is simple, and because it is so simple, few people find it. All you have to do is know where you are going and what you want. Set your goal, and go after it, keeping your mind on the things you want and off the things you don't want. Create a burning desire for the things you want. Learn to change the negative thoughts that enter your mind (the things you don't want) to positive thoughts (the things you want): "For what I fear comes upon me, and what I dread befalls me" (Job 3:25 NEW AMERICAN STANDARD BIBLE); "Ask, and it shall be given you; seek, and ye shall find; knock, and it shall be opened unto you" (Matthew 7:7 KING JAMES VERSION); and "Remember this: The person who plants a little will have a small harvest, but the person who plants a lot will have a big harvest. Each one should give as you have decided in your heart to give. You should not be sad when you give, and you should not give because you feel forced to give. God loves the person who gives happily. And God can give you more blessings than you need. Then you will always have plenty of everything— enough to give to every good work" (2 Corinthians 9:6-8 NEW CENTURY VERSION).

In The Greatest Salesman in the World, Og Mandino says, "Failure will never overtake me if my determination to succeed is strong enough." He also says, citing an idea that goes back at least to Aristotle, "When an act becomes easy through constant repetition it becomes a pleasure to perform and if it is a pleasure to perform it is man's nature to perform it often. When I perform it often it becomes a habit and I become its slave and since it is a good habit this is my will."

When good habits are repeated, they become easy, and success is certain. If you incorporate that philosophy into your business and life, you will see greater returns and rewards than you ever imagined: "I can do all things through Christ who strengthens me" (Philippians 4:13 NEW KING JAMES VERSION), and "The measure you give will be the measure you get back" (Luke 6:38 NEW REVISED STANDARD VERSION).

As you go about your daily work, learn to stay positive by making positive statements out loud: "When the going gets tough, the tough get going." "Day by day in every way I'm getting better and better." And "what the mind of man can conceive and believe, it can achieve."

Here are a few more positive affirmations I've gathered over the years:

BELIEVE AND ACHIEVE
- Feed your subconscious mind with positive thoughts.
- You must have a dream if you are going to make a dream come true.
- Go power = positive mental attitude. Do it now!
- Thoughts are powerful when they are mixed with definiteness of purpose, persistence, and a burning desire for their achievement.
- If you do not see riches in your imagination, you will never see them in your bank balance.
- Your brain becomes magnetized by the dominating thoughts you hold in your mind.
- Desire is the starting point of all achievements.
- You must be able to visualize your desired goal.

- Keep on visualizing your desired goal until it becomes a burning desire, as if your life depended on it.
- You are never defeated until you accept defeat.
- Every adversity brings with it the seeds of an equivalent advantage.
- Believe, believe, and believe in the power of desire backed by faith and action.

To keep a positive mental attitude, I recommend that you make a copy of these positive statements, keep it handy and read it out loud—often! You will be amazed at the results.

Chapter 40

Goals: Knowing Where You're Going

*Success is tied to service
in any business-related enterprise.
More service equals more success.*

Almost nothing has had a more profound impact on my life than inspirational literature. From the day Jack Schooley introduced me to it, the writing of authors like Napoleon Hill and Frank Bettger has shaped my thought process and helped guide me to success.

I have always been willing to work hard. I have always had a desire to provide well for my family and not to be poor. But until I first heard and understood Earl Nightingale and followed the path set out by him and those other authors, I didn't have a way to put it all together.

To this day, they shape the way I think. I'd be afraid to guess how many times through the years I've taken *Think and Grow Rich* down from the shelf and read the chapter on faith. Whenever I get down and out, what I call having the blahs, I read that chapter, and I can feel the hair on the back of my neck raise up a little bit. I tell people all the time, "If that doesn't make you want to go out and accomplish something, you need to get a job at a service station."

Think and Grow Rich offers a formula for self-confidence that I have adhered to since I first read it. I repeated it aloud every morning throughout my career, and I still find it to be a great summary of the attitude of success. I quoted it early in the book, but it is such an important part of my story that I want to quote it again:

> *"I fully realize that no wealth or position can long endure unless built upon truth and justice. Therefore I will engage in no transaction which does not benefit all whom it affects. I will succeed by attracting to myself the forces I wish to use, and the cooperation of other people. I will induce others to serve me because of my willingness to serve others. I will eliminate hatred, envy, jealousy, selfishness and cynicism by developing love for all humanity because I know that a negative attitude towards others can never bring me success. I will cause others to believe in me, because I will believe in them, and in myself. I will sign my name to this formula, commit it to memory and repeat it aloud once a day, with full faith that it will gradually influence my thoughts and actions so that I will become a self-reliant and successful person."**

---

* *Excerpt from* Think and Grow Rich, *by Napoleon Hill, is used with the consent of the Napoleon Hill Foundation. Information about the Foundation can be found at www.naphill.org.*

I did what it suggested, and it did what it promised.

All of us have the potential for success and achievement, but far too many of us get distracted or discouraged. Too many of us never give serious thought to why we're here. We never study how we might achieve the dreams all of us have for a better life, a life where service and usefulness lead to success and happiness.

When I say success, by the way, I'm not talking just about money or other signs of economic or business accomplishments; I'm talking about success at life, things like love and happiness, faith, and good relations with people.

When it comes to all of those things, it is what we carry around in our heads that is the key. If I had a motto, it would be, "You are what you think." If your head is full of defeat, doubt, and fear, you don't have a chance at success.

This quote, whose original source is obscure, sums up a lot for me:

Watch your thoughts, for they become words.

Watch your words, for they become actions.

Watch your actions, for they become habits.

Watch your habits, for they become character.

Watch your character, for it becomes your destiny.

We are all responsible for taking whatever natural traits and talents we have and turning them into a useful and productive life. I've never found clearer, more useful instructions for accomplishing that than in the inspirational literature of the twentieth century. I had never been much of a reader. I wasn't very good at it, and it really didn't interest me. Jack Schooley changed all that. By introducing me to *Think and Grow Rich*, he got me started on a path I'm still walking today. I've read inspirational books and collected inspirational quotes from then on, and to this day I hardly ever read anything that isn't designed to fire me up and make me better at the art of living. I believe that in order to be enthusiastic, you've got to act enthusiastically. Reading motivational books helped me do just that. It helped me to keep a positive attitude and to keep my eye on my goal. It gave me confidence that I could reach my goal—any goal.

Frank Bettger's *How I Raised Myself from Failure to Success in Selling* had a huge influence on me as well. Its lessons for success came straight out of Bettger's life, and I could relate to him because he had been where I was. He was a salesman who sometimes had to face down fear and self-doubt, just as I had. He told one story of arriving at the office of the president of a large New York manufacturing company seeking $250,000 of life insurance. When he walked in, the president showed him a stack of proposals from other agents, some of them close friends and golfing buddies.

"I'm afraid you're wasting your time," he told Bettger.

His comment was designed to discourage Bettger, and it would have worked on most salesmen. But Bettger wasn't discouraged. He knew the insurance was necessary for securing a $250,000 loan—that the creditor had full faith in the president, but not in his company should he be incapacitated. He told the president as much and said that if he were to come down with so much as a cold, it could delay the insurance and the loan and have a major negative impact on the company. Then he said he had made an appointment for the president to be examined by a medical examiner whose report would satisfy any insurer and clear the way for the policy—and the loan. The president was impressed enough to keep the appointment and take the policy.

"Mr. Bettger," he asked, "whom do you represent?"

"I represent you!" was the answer.

When Bettger was young, he played baseball. Early on, he was accused of being lazy, and he decided that was never going to happen again. He began hustling everywhere he went. He brought all the energy he had to everything he did. He went so far that everyone began calling him "Pep" Bettger.

He first worked in the insurance business at Fidelity Mutual Life Insurance Company, and he had decided after "ten miserable, disheartening months" to resign. As he was cleaning out his desk, the company president called a sales meeting, and he was too embarrassed to leave. At the meeting, he heard the president say, "This business of selling narrows down to one thing...seeing the people! Show me any man of ordinary ability who will go out and earnestly tell his story to four or five people every day, and I will show you a man who just can't help making good!"

Bettger realized he hadn't given the business real effort, and he was fired up enough by the president's pep talk to try. Once he did, everything turned around, and he became a success in the business he had been ready to quit.

Reading stories like that motivated me to no end. Knowing Bettger and those others had succeeded led me to believe that I could do it too.

Through the years I read Zig Ziglar, Dale Carnegie, Robert Schuller, and many others, but the foundation of my success has always rested on two works—Napoleon Hill's *Think and Grow Rich* and Earl Nightingale's *The Strangest Secret*. They taught and inspired me. When I met resistance, when I felt down, I would think about what the record or the book had to say, and I would be lifted up.

I remember the Saturday morning when I taped Jack's copy of *The Strangest Secret* onto an early cassette I could play in my car. As I did, my son Randy, who was eight or nine, came running through the house, and Sadie hollered at him, "Quit running through this house!" Through the years I heard her yell that hundreds of times as I listened to that tape again and again.

Think and Grow Rich is a textbook, something worth studying, and I've always treated it that way. I've read it many times, and I've given copies or recommended it to hundreds of people through the years.

"If you want riches," Hill wrote, "you must refuse to accept any circumstance that leads toward poverty, and avoid thoughts that focus on poverty." He counseled against even the fear of poverty, since it would keep the concept of poverty in your head.

Hill emphasized the need for persistence and self-discipline. He was one of the earliest proponents of a concept that Nike later picked up on and boiled down to three words: *Just do it*. When it comes to doing the right thing on any subject—from work to fitness to charity—you can't just think about it. You have to take action, and it's got to become automatic. If you think about it, it's too easy to talk yourself out of it. That's what self-discipline is all about.

"There are four simple steps," Hill wrote, "which lead to the habit of persistence. They call for no great amount of intelligence, no particular amount of education and but little time or effort. The necessary steps are:

1. A definite purpose backed by a burning desire for its fulfillment.
2. A definite plan, expressed in continuous action.
3. A mind closed tightly against all negative and discouraging influences, including negative suggestions of relatives, friends and acquaintances.
4. A friendly alliance with one or more persons who will encourage you to follow through with both plan and purpose.

"These four steps are essential for success in all walks of life."

Persistence is evident in all sorts of successful endeavors. I remember a piece on Babe Ruth called "The Biggest Failure in Baseball." He may have hit 714 home runs, but Ruth struck out 1,330 times in his career. The piece had a photo of Ruth with his bat, and it talked about an interview he did when he was in a batting slump. "How do you feel knowing you haven't had a hit in all those times at bat?" the reporter asked him.

Ruth said, "I just keep standing up there and taking those healthy swings. I know that if I keep doing my best, eventually I'm going to make a connection."

I always advised my salesmen that when you look at the guys who are the great successes in life, you've got to understand that they failed too. Life is about learning to overcome those failures and use them as stepping-stones to success. That's the way

I used every failure I faced—as a stepping-stone. Earl Nightingale started that great record of his by talking about the fact that the vast majority of people fail in terms of where they end up versus what they dreamed of becoming. I didn't want to be one of those people.

We are constantly feeding our minds, and we need to do so responsibly. If you don't feed your body properly, you'll get sick. If you don't feed your mind properly, it will stagnate. You'll get to thinking negatively instead of positively. Success lies in switching those negative thoughts to positive thoughts, and that's almost impossible to do without a conscious goal. Most people fail because they don't have a goal. They have no idea where they're going. When you know where you're going, when you have a goal, and something negative creeps into your mind, you have something to shift your thoughts to. It's so important to keep your mind off the things you don't want and on the things you do want, and a big part of that is being around people who are going to encourage you to do the right thing because it's the right thing to do.

The people who succeed are those who decide, "This is what I want to do," set their goal, and go after it single-mindedly. You've got to put your blinders on. You can't do one thing well if you're doing a dozen others at the same time. Your goal has to take priority. I divided my goal into short- and long-term components. The long-term goal involved security for me and my family—money in the bank, a nice home and car, and a few luxuries. How would I get there? That's where the short-term goals came in. Day in and day out I had to render service, give people their money's

worth in terms of the insurance policies I sold. If I
wanted more money in the long run, I had to give
more service in the short run. It was that simple.

Success is tied to service in any business-related
enterprise. More service equals more success. A
lot of people get tripped up there because service
takes work. It's easier to think negatively because
you can do that sitting down. Thinking positively
requires acting positively. I have to do something.
"Always do more than you're paid for," Hill says in
Think and Grow Rich, and I've found that practice
to be a key engine of success.

I have caught myself starting to become negative
many times in my life. When that happens, I close
my eyes and picture an electrical outlet. I'll reach
over and I'll unplug the negative, then turn it over to
where it's positive and plug it back in. I concentrate
on that image. That will help me to shift my thinking
back to my goal. *How am I going to get back on track
toward reaching my goal?* I would say to myself,
and in three or four minutes of concentration, I
could always bring back that positive energy. Then
I would set my sights on doing something good for
someone else.

Say I hadn't made a sale all day. I might think,
*I'm going to stop selling insurance and start visiting
with people. I'm going to be the most enthusiastic
person they have ever met. They are going to
remember me because I'm going to be excited about
meeting them. I'm going to grab that hand and say,
"How in the world are you doing?" and they are
going to be impressed by me.*

Invariably, I'd find someone to talk to, and I'd
end up making a sale. I've had days where at three
o'clock in the afternoon I hadn't sold a thing, and
my attitude began to take on a negative charge.

I'd stop and unplug that connection and plug it back into a positive one, then pump myself up and take that positive energy to someone. I'd make a sale and then ask them to tell me someone else who needed a good policy like the one I'd just sold them. I'd visit that next person and the next. And I'd be driving home finally at nine or ten o'clock that night, feeling something I can only describe as spiritual.

"Thank you, Lord, for seeing me through one more time," I'd pray. I bet I've done that a thousand times. And I learned how to do it, how to trade failure for success, negative for positive, pessimism for optimism, in the words of Napoleon Hill and Earl Nightingale and all the rest. I'm grateful for them every day, as I am for the Bible verse I repeat so often: "For as he thinketh in his heart, so is he" (Proverbs 23:7 KING JAMES VERSION).

Chapter 41

The Joy Of Giving

The building is called
the Randall and Sadie Baskin Center.

Growing up, I had the best example of giving I could ever want right in my own home. It came in the form of my sister Betty, who took $1.50 of the $13.00 she got every week from her job at the drugstore and gave it to Marion and me so we could pay for lunch at school.

I've tried all my life to live up to her example. If I see somebody who needs something, I help out.

My own charitable giving isn't the kind of thing I would usually talk about, but Rob Simbeck, who helped me turn my memories into this book, said it would be good to give people a look at that side of me—that it would remind them of the importance of giving and of the true joy that it brings.

Giving has never been something I've spent a lot of time thinking about. I just follow my heart; it tells me when I need to give. Through the years I have given away millions of dollars, but it was a process that started slowly. Early on, there wasn't much to give. But in the years since, I have succeeded in business and in life beyond any dream I've ever had. I have talked in this book about some of the material rewards of that success, but along the way I've learned that real fulfillment comes from sharing that wealth and that success. I have been able to know the true joy of giving, something I hope everyone gets to experience.

That's always been true on a family level—perhaps too much so. There are ways where I can see how I've spoiled my boys and some of my grandkids. It was just always hard to say no. In recent years as I've structured my estate, I've wanted to make sure they're taken care of, but in a way that doesn't just give them fish but that encourages them to keep fishing. And through the Foundation I've established, I want to do even more for others, for those outside my family who are in real need. I want to help mankind.

Maybe because we were so poor, I've always had a soft spot for poor kids. One year my brother Art and I decided to visit the Baptist Children's Home and see what we might do for the kids' Christmas. We decided on a "Christmas adoption," where everybody would bring a child or two home and give them Christmas there.

Then, in the late 1980s, Cumberland House, which housed and educated about forty kids who'd been abused, sexually or otherwise, contacted me. They knew about my giving and asked if I could help them. The state had cut their funding, and they were in a tough spot. I got my employees at Continental involved and told them I'd match whatever contributions they made. They really immersed themselves in the joy of giving. They started doing bake sales and other fund-raisers all through the year, and all the money went into a Christmas fund for those kids. We'd get a wish list from each child, and I'd have a couple of employees from different departments go at different times to do the shopping. Then we'd bring the kids—forty or fifty of them—to our headquarters and throw a big party, complete with a visit from Santa Claus. We'd feed them and give them goodie bags with clothes and toys and other surprises. To watch those kids open those bags we'd loaded with gifts was really something. It was a joyful occasion for all of us. We did that for thirteen years, moving the party to the Cumberland House itself after a few years, and when we had extra funds built up, we'd buy a computer or something else for them.

I've been a big supporter of Franklin Road Academy, a private school in Nashville. Roger and his wife, Lisa, two of my grandsons, Austin and Trevor, and my nephew Mike Baskin have all graduated from there. When the school needs money for furniture or the library, I'm glad to help out, and when it undertook its last building program seven years ago, I donated $250,000 to build the tower attached to the school's library.

A few years back, Sadie and I began visiting Brentwood Baptist Church, pastored by Mike Glenn, a man who's done great work in his fifteen years there. His sermon one Sunday inspired me enough that as I put a check for $1,000 in the basket, I decided I needed to write another to help meet a need he had talked about. I took a check from my billfold and wrote another for $5,000. When we joined the church, I began giving $5,000 a week. Brentwood Baptist now has something like eighty-five hundred members. Mike's done a wonderful job with the church in general and with its young people in particular. His Tuesday night services for young adults draw huge crowds every week.

After we'd been members for quite a while, Mike came to me about building a 250-seat chapel for weddings, funerals, concerts, and services that don't require the 2,000-seat main worship center. He asked if I would consider funding it. I pledged $3 million and was very proud and happy when the chapel was dedicated in December 2009. When the church was going to eliminate the steeple because of cost, I increased my commitment by $375,000 to cover it. Construction on the tower took about eight months, and it is now in place and looks wonderful. The tower has chimes that play every hour on the hour, and the sound is beautiful.

The plaque says:

"The Baskin Chapel of Brentwood Baptist Church is dedicated to the glory of God and the memory of Randall R. Baskin, Jr. (Randy) by Randall R. Baskin, Sr. and his wife, Sadie.

"Randy went to be with the Lord as a result of a tragic automobile accident on November 23, 1991. He was a member of Radnor Baptist Church in Nashville, Tennessee.

"This chapel also honors the Baskins' other son, Roger S. Baskin and their five grandsons: Randall R. Baskin, III (Rafe), Blake Baskin, Stefan Baskin, sons of Randy and Tammy Baskin; Austin Baskin and Trevor Baskin, sons of Roger and Lisa Baskin.

"The Baskin Chapel is especially designed to serve the members of Brentwood Baptist Church, their families and friends, and to honor our Lord and Savior, Jesus Christ.

"Randall and Sadie pray that the chapel will inspire and encourage others to share their love for Christ with each other and to glorify His kingdom.

"God originally designed the world for good. We were created to have a relationship with Him and with each other. Genesis 1:31."

I still keep in touch with Radnor Baptist, which is now known as Sunset Hills Baptist. My friend Paul Durham died several years ago, and his son Steve Durham is now the pastor. When the congregation wanted to erect a new church building, I issued a challenge—if they raised $100,000 toward the building fund, I would match it. They finished raising the money in the fall of 2011, and on Sunday, December 18, 2011, Sadie and I, along with Rafe and his girlfriend Anna, visited the church. I presented a check for $100,000 to Steve and expressed my appreciation to the congregation, telling them how exciting it was for me to be there in the church where I first learned the joy of giving as a young man. I congratulated everyone who had made a commitment toward the $100,000, and the appreciation expressed by so many members of the congregation afterward was very gratifying.

There are a lot of organizations I support. I've given to the Fannie Battle Day Home and the children of the Middle Tennessee Mental Health Institute, as well as St. Jude Children's Research Hospital, Mercy Children's Clinic, and Nashville-area programs called Brightstone and Saddle Up. We supported Dream Makers, which had a celebrity waiter luncheon every year. There, we could get up close with the likes of Reba McEntire,

Randy Travis, and Stella Parton. I know the good work Scouting does, too, and the good influence it has on kids, and I donate to Scouting to this day.

You don't have to look very far to find people in desperate need. I donate to food banks and missions that help the poor and homeless, and I'm a big believer in the work the Salvation Army does year in and year out, especially at Christmas. There have also been many times through the years when I've seen something in the paper or on TV, and my heart will tell me to do something. There's no telling what will trigger it, and I tend to be very spur of the moment about it. I always say that if my heart tells me to do something, I do it quick, before the devil talks me out of it, and I've never helped anybody that I wish I hadn't.

A couple of years ago I was watching TV when they showed a Methodist church collecting toys to give to needy children who slip through the cracks of other charitable agencies. The camera panned the room that was supposed to hold the toys people brought, and it was empty. I took down the address, and the next day I wrote a check for $5,000, drove there, and gave it to the preacher. I don't think he'd ever seen that much money, and he was really appreciative.

When Nashville was hit with big floods in the spring of 2010, a business owned by the daughter of good friends of mine was wiped out. I took a generator and some supplies over when the water subsided and gave her $10,000 to help out. She was renting the building from her parents, and I couldn't get them out of my mind. Finally I went by their house and left them a check for $10,000. Her mother hugged my neck out of joy and relief, and later she called again to thank me, stopping every now and then to cry. Then Sadie and I got a thank-you card and note from her daughter that made both of us cry.

Another time, not long ago, as Sadie and I were drinking coffee and reading the newspaper, she said, "You need to read this story." A team of doctors had operated on this child's heart but weren't able to repair it the way they'd hoped. His name was Witt, and he needed a transplant. I put the paper in my briefcase, and when I got to the office, I called the child's grandmother. I told her I was going to send her a check for $5,000. She thanked me profusely, and I went in to my secretary, Shirley, and said, "Write them a check for five thousand dollars."

I went back to the office, stopped, and turned around.

"No, Shirley," I said. "Write it for ten."

I called the lady back and said, "I've had a change of heart. I'm sending ten."

"Ten dollars?" she said.

"No, ten thousand."

"My son's standing right here," she said. "Let me let you talk to him."

He told me how very grateful he was, and later his wife and the Heart Association called and thanked me too. They put the boy on a transplant list, and finally he received a heart. A week or so later his grandmother sent a letter with a picture and told me he was doing fine. I sat there reading the letter with big old tears rolling down my cheeks.

"I'm so thankful that God brought us together," she wrote, and I wrote back and told her I was glad too. To this day, we keep up with Witt's progress, and his parents call me whenever they're in town.

Belmont University approached me again a few

years back asking if I would consider building a law school. My relationship with Belmont goes back to 1979, when I was asked to join the board. Soon afterward I established a scholarship fund, which now totals about $400,000, with the interest going to help students. The school told me not long ago that the fund has helped more than a hundred students get their education.

I said yes to the law school idea. We talked about the building that would house it, and I pledged $7 million toward its completion. I pictured what it might look like, the way I used to picture the nice house I wanted to build on my father's property back before Sadie and I moved off to Nashville. Then, during the groundbreaking ceremony on October 14, 2010, I talked about looking over the plans the architect had drawn up.

"I've been building this in my mind for a number of years," I said, "and the thing I can't understand is how Earl Swensson Associates could read my mind and come up with a building that was almost exactly what I had imagined." Everyone laughed, but a few days later Earl Swensson's office called to ask for permission to use what I'd said for their own public relations. The building is called the Randall and Sadie Baskin Center, and it opened August 21, 2012. It's one of the things I'm proudest of.

I've always believed that what you put out is what you get back, and I had a nearly literal experience of that after I pledged the money for the law school. The commitment I made was for $1 million a year for seven years. Just after I made it, my broker, James Nichols, came to talk to me about one of my investments.

"I've been looking at the $10 million bond you

284 GROWING RICH: Success in Business, Success in Life

bought a couple of years ago," he said, "and you could sell it at a pretty good profit." In fact, I could sell it for $720,000 more than I paid for it. As he was talking, it hit me that I hadn't made the first payment to Belmont yet, and here I could sell a bond and earn almost enough to cover it. It was the largest single financial decision I'd ever made, and the first part of it was almost replaced before I ever paid it. I don't do things for that reason, but I invariably find that when I give, I get. It's not always or even usually money. It's usually joy in hearing from someone whose life is a little better or someone whose gratitude just makes my day. One example of that came from the parents of the boy who had the heart operation. They sent me a card with a photo, and I hung it on the refrigerator around Thanksgiving, when I knew the whole family would be stopping by. I wanted all of them to receive that blessing with me.

I had another large bond that I sold for $300,000 more than I paid for it, and it had earned $300,000 in interest, for a total of $600,000. Recently I sold one for $182,780 more than I paid for it, and it had been earning 4 percent interest for two years. James advised me that my total earnings on the $1 million bond were 22 percent after taxes for a little more than two years.

I know I've given away a lot of money through the years—as I said, my heart leads me and I do it. Sadie can be a little more cautious about such things, and one night as we were driving home after I'd pledged my big Belmont donation, she said, "We can't keep up Radnor Baptist Church and Belmont University. You're just giving money away like crazy."

I thought about it, and that night as we lay in

bed in the dark, I said, "Honey, I want to have a little talk with you." Things got quiet. I said, "I've got a confession I want to make to you."

"What's that?"

"For years, I've heard you talk more times than I can count about how hard I work, and I agree, I do work hard. But I want to confess to you, Honey, I'm not that good. I've had a lot of help along the way. I've got thousands of people under contract. Every time they make a sale it puts money in my pocket. If my life depended on it, I couldn't call three percent of them by name. I don't know them. But they're part of this big company that makes my living and a whole lot more. And there's one thing you've got to understand. When my heart tells me to do something, I'm going to do it. Think back to those days when you and I were lying in that little trailer. Think about that night when there was water dripping on us in bed, and we moved to the other end of the trailer and it leaked on us there too. Stop and think about how appreciative we should be that we've come from there to here, that we live in a place like we live in. All the goodness that we've had in our lives is enough to make me want to help somebody else, and that's what I'm going to do."

Well, I guess that talk really sank in because she's never said another word.

In fact, I'm grateful for every opportunity I've had to do something that has helped another. I want the world to be a better place because I lived, and I know that part of how I can make that happen is with charitable giving. The Lord has blessed me financially, and being able to pass those blessings on has been a great joy. It's one of the ways I feel most connected with people and with the Lord.

Chapter 42

The Greatest Riches

*"It's what you put in the life of others
that comes back to your very own."*

Jesus said to him, "If you wish to be complete,
go and sell your possessions and give to the poor,
and you will have treasure in heaven; and come,
follow Me."
—Matthew 19:21 New American Standard Bible

I hope you've seen that although I've been
blessed with a great deal of worldly wealth, I've
learned that there is much greater treasure
than what can be measured monetarily. Giving
money to those in need has greatly increased
my awareness of this greater treasure, and
that awareness has grown into a much deeper
understanding in my spirit, like yeast expanding
in warm bread. I've come to realize that giving to
others from these greater, eternal riches—what
might be called treasures in Heaven—gives you
a joy that beats even that of giving a check for a
million dollars! And anyone can do it, no matter
what size bank account they have!

By now you know that my faith in biblical principles has guided my way and helped me succeed in overcoming great obstacles. The Golden Rule that Jesus taught is the real foundation for the wisdom of Earl Nightingale, Napoleon Hill, Norman Vincent Peale, and many of the motivational teachers who shaped my thinking and my career. You could say that my life has been a journey of practicing my faith, always asking God for direction to do the right thing.

Not long ago, something happened that showed me that giving to others from these greatest of riches can release truly miraculous blessings for everyone involved. It allowed me to share my faith in a way I never had before, and I wanted to close with that story.

For several years, Sadie and I have gone to our condo in Florida to attend the Panama City horse show, held the last week of April. In 2012, it was to start April 26th, and we made our plans to go to the condo about a week earlier.

I went to the office a little early that morning to finish up some last-minute business before leaving town. My very good friend Bobby called and said that he wanted to have lunch with me and that he would pick me up at 11:30. I have known Bobby for several years; in fact, I had the privilege of seeing him go in business for himself and become very successful. He always seemed to look to me for advice and always paid close attention to what I had to say. He was a hard worker, and from time to time I did spend a good bit of time motivating him.

When he picked me up, I could tell that something was wrong. He told me that he had a fast-growing tumor in his pancreas, and the doctor felt certain it was cancerous. He had already taken two doses of chemo. Some of the hair on the back of his head was coming out.

"Randall, have you ever felt like you are going to die?" he asked. "Well, I feel I am going to die."

I was so upset about his negative frame of mind that I didn't want to leave town. But I knew Sadie's heart was set on leaving, and I knew I could pray for my good friend just as well in Florida as I could here, so we loaded the Prevost motor coach and headed south, my mind dead set on Bobby as I drove. We arrived in Birmingham about 9:30 p.m. and decided to spend the night at our favorite place, the Flying J, part of a chain of truck stops.

I wouldn't describe myself as an overly religious person, but faith has played a huge part in my life's story. Now, my friend's faith and his trust in me for guidance seemed to put me to a real test, one that I've never experienced before.

For several years, I have been saving Bible verses, most recently in the note pad of my iPhone. I keep those that touch me most and read them again from time to time. They always give me direction that helps me do the best with my opportunities as well as the extra strength to handle the tragedies that life sometimes brings. I find some of these verses as I read other motivational books, but the majority come from my regular reading of the Bible.

I never thought about them being as useful as they were on this occasion. As soon as we got parked, I started going through these verses with my friend in mind. I then sent him a text message with a Bible verse and my instructions, as follows:

Jesus said unto him, "If thou canst, believe all things are possible to him that believeth." Mark 9:23 . . . Bobby; pray like you've never prayed before. Ask God to heal you. Then shift your thinking to as positive as you can be, and tell yourself that you will be all right. You must believe. Make positive statements: "Day by day in every way I'm getting better and better." Do this over and over, and keep this in your mind. Say it again and again, and the faith will come to you . . . and you will believe! You Must Believe. God Bless. I'm praying for you.

The next morning, I woke up at 5:00 a.m. and just lay there thinking and asking God to heal and guide my friend through his very serious problem. I eased out of bed, trying not to wake Sadie, and started looking for another good Bible verse. After a while, I sent this one:

April 19, 2012 6:24 a.m.
"Therefore I tell you whatever you ask for in prayer, believe that you will receive it and it will be yours." Mark 11:24

After sending that text, I made coffee. Sadie got up, and we had breakfast and took our showers. I cranked up the Prevost, checked my tow car, and we headed south on I-65. After driving several hours, we stopped at a roadside park to take a break and send my friend another Bible verse:

April 19, 2012 2:39 p.m.
"If you have faith as a grain of mustard seed nothing shall be impossible unto you." Matthew 17:20

After I sent that message, I found more verses

that stirred my heart, uplifting messages I felt my friend could hold onto. They were in a very real sense messages from his Creator that were helping to save his life.

We arrived at the condo, unloaded the coach, got moved in, and went out for dinner. After returning to the condo, I found several more good Bible verses before retiring for the night. I was amazed at the number of messages from the Word I was finding related to asking and receiving. Before retiring that night I got a call from Bobby, and he said, "Keep those Bible verses coming!"

So I did:

April 19, 2012 8:22 p.m.

"Be strong and of good courage; do not be afraid, nor be dismayed, for the Lord your God is with you wherever you go." Josh 1:9 . . . "For as he thinketh in his heart, so is he." Proverbs 23:7

I received the following "thank you" text from my friend, and immediately sent him another quote.

April 19, 2012 9:04 p.m.

"If God is for us, who can be against us?" Rom. 8:31

Reply dated April 19, 2012 9:16 p.m.

"Thank you so much for your prayers, Randall. I feel so much better. With you and God on my side I can't help but be healthy."

April 19, 2012 9:16 p.m.

"For everyone that asketh receiveth, and he that seeketh findeth; and to him that knocketh it shall be open." Matthew 7:8

Another day, and I was still looking for the

right uplifting quotes for my friend. For some reason I was feeling better about him. I could tell from talking to him and reading his text message that he, too, was much better and had a positive attitude. So I was determined to keep them coming:

With tears swirling my vision, I managed to peck out the verse I had found to send to Bobby:

April 20, 2012 10:25 a.m.
"Give all your worries to him, because he cares about you." 1 Peter 5:7

April 20, 2012 11:12 a.m.
"Jesus said to her, I am the resurrection, and the life: he that believeth in me, though he was dead, yet shall he live and whosoever liveth and believeth in me shall never die. Believeth thou this?" John 11:25-26

The next day I continued looking for and sending more Bible verses:

April 21, 2012 12:09 p.m.
"Faith means being sure of the things we hope for and knowing that something is real even if we do not see it." Hebrews 11:1-2

April 21, 2012 12:35 p.m.
"For God has not given us a spirit of fear, but of power and of love and of sound mind." 2 Timothy 1:7

And then:

April 24, 2012 9:27 p.m.
"By the way, Bobby . . . Are you still feeling good?

Followed soon after by:

Reply dated April 24, 2012:
"Yes. Feeling great."

And so it went for the rest of the week, with many, many more messages of hope. Hope is, to my mind, one of the most beautiful words in the New Testament: "And now abideth faith, hope, love" (1 Corinthians 13:13). Then a few days later, it came . . . the message we had all been hoping for:

Reply dated April 27, 2012:
"Your prayers, and mine were answered today. The surgeon removed a 5cm cyst today weighing just over one pound. He is as certain as one can be that this procedure got all of it. An immediate biopsy of it determined it benign. I am resting well and will be 100% by Monday."

Holding back tears, I managed to reply:

April 27, 2012 7:31 p.m.
"Don't forget to thank God."

He promptly replied:

April 27:
"Oh believe me . . . I thank God." Then he added; "I think you have a direct line to the man upstairs. Thank goodness cause I needed all the help I could get."

We left Panama City May 1st after the horse show and drove to New Orleans to attend a motor coach rally and didn't return home until May 7th. The following week I had lunch with my good friend again. This time I saw a new person, a friend with a smile on his face and a twinkle in his eyes, a person with a new lease on life. He explained to me that, on the day we had lunch, weeks before, when he dropped me off at my office, he'd gotten to the next intersection and found himself lost. He said it took a while to decide which way to turn. He also recalled that as he drove home that afternoon, he noticed more than ever the beauty of nature, trees, and greenery that he hadn't seen before. Then, with tears in his eyes, he thanked me for the Bible verses. I thought back to that day he had called me and said, "Keep them coming, please." He explained to me how each one seemed to be just what he needed at the time. I estimated that I probably sent him thirty Bible verses. He responded, "No, you sent me thirty-six!"*

Bobby had promised me he would be in church with me the following Sunday. That Sunday, he texted me and said that his daughter called and was taking her new baby to church for the first time and wanted him to go with her. I understood and thought that would be even better.

We had lunch again the following week, and he told me about sharing his experience about his cancer scare with the preacher at the daughter's church and about the big part I played with the Bible text messages. He said he got so emotional he got to crying and even had the preacher crying. The preacher wanted to meet me and wanted to use the story in one of his sermons. He asked my friend to come and tell his story to the church.

Bobby shared with me that he was having the texts laminated and framed and was getting three of them made so he could give one to me and one to the preacher.

I have never experienced such a spiritual feeling as I felt in helping my friend through the darkest days of his life with those uplifting verses—those treasures from Heaven. I never realized I had

---

* I didn't include all thirty-six verses in this final chapter, but you can download them yourself by going to www.GrowingRichBook.com

recorded so many Bible verses in my phone that would be so helpful for an occasion like this. It was like God had guided me during the last three years in putting them in my phone to be used for this occasion. Yes, I had advised my friend to be sure to thank God. And I have also thanked Him for allowing me to be a part of this wonderful experience, one like no other I've ever had before.

While still working on the final chapter of this book, I awoke one Sunday morning to receive a very nice text from my friend Bobby:

> June 17 2012 8:57 a.m.
>
> "Happy Father's Day!!! Thank you so much for being the Father and mentor to me that I never had. You shaped my life over the last two decades to make me a better father and a better person. Most important you've taught me the value of faith in God and the power of prayer."

As I read this text from my friend, the words became hazy to the point I could hardly see. My eyes were so full of tears of joy that they ran down both cheeks. Without a doubt, this is the greatest compliment I've ever received, and I thank God for giving me the courage and faith to help my friend. I realized through that Father's Day message, the greatest joy had come from sharing those heavenly treasures from our Eternal Father, and I thanked Him again for the blessing He made possible for us all. It is so true: our greatest riches of life come from within. I don't think there is any truer statement than "it's what you put in the life of others that comes back to your very own."

———∞∞∞———

I've tried to use the story of my journey from poverty to riches, from want to security, as a means of passing on the lessons I've learned along the way. The final one is both a lesson and a wish. It is summed up in a line from the Prayer of St. Francis: "It is by giving that we receive." I have received more blessings from giving than from anything else I have ever done. You can too. May you know the joy of giving.

Books Mentioned In

GROWING RICH:
Success in Business,
Success in Life

Think and Grow Rich* — Napoleon Hill

Gleanings — A. M. Burton

The Shack — William D. Young

The Strangest Secret (audio recording) — Earl Nightingale

How I Raised Myself from Failure to Success in Selling — Frank Bettger

The Secret; The Power — Rhonda Byrne

The Richest Man in Babylon — George Samuel Clason

How to Win Friends and Influence People — Dale Carnegie

---

* *Excerpt from* Think and Grow Rich, *by Napoleon Hill, is used with the consent of the Napoleon Hill Foundation. Information about the Foundation can be found at www.naphill.org.*

Other Books
That Have Inspired Me

Your Magic Power to Be Rich; Napoleon Hill's Golden Rules; What Would Napoleon Hill Do?; Success Through a Positive Mental Attitude; Grow Rich! With Peace of Mind; Think and Grow Rich in a Minute; How to Sell Your Way Through Life; The Magic Ladder to Success; The Master Key to Riches — Napoleon Hill

The True Joy of Positive Living; The Power of Positive Thinking — Dr. Norman Vincent Peale

Led to Follow — J. Howard Olds and Cal Turner, Jr.

Daughter of the Air — Rob Simbeck

In Real Time; The Power of Yes — Mike Glenn

The Choice; Og Mandino's Great Trilogy: The Greatest Salesman in the World, The Greatest Secret in the World, the Greatest Miracle in the World; The Twelfth Angel — Og Mandino

Taking Care of eBusiness — Thomas M. Siebel

Don't Grow Old ...Grow Up! — Dorothy Carnegie

Is It Worth Dying For? — Dr. Robert S. Eliot and Dennis L. Breo

The Skyline Is a Promise — Guilford Dudley, Jr.

The Art of Public Speaking — Dale Carnegie

See You at the Top; Zig Ziglar's Secrets of Closing the Sale; Confessions of a Happy Christian — Zig Ziglar

Running — James Fixx

A Flock of Eagles — Quaife M. Ward and Tedd Determan

The Winner's Edge — Denis Waitley

How to Live 365 Days a Year — John A. Schindler, M.D.

Law of Attraction — Michael J. Losier

Ask and It Is Given — Esther and Jerry Hicks

The 100 Absolutely Unbreakable Laws of Business Success — Brian Tracy

The Secret of Happiness — Billy Graham

Sarah — Kaylene Johnson

The Success Principles — Jack Canfield

Buffett — Roger Lowenstein

Secret of Greatness — editors of Fortune magazine

Life Is a Gift — Bob and Judy Fisher

Awakening to Your Life's Purpose; The Power of Now; A New Earth — Eckhart Tolle

The Purpose Driven Life; God's Answers to Life's Difficult Questions — Rick Warren

The Little Gold Book of Yes! Attitude — Jeffrey Gitomer

Who Moved My Cheese? — Spencer Johnson, M.D.

The One Minute Sales Person — Spencer Johnson and Larry Wilson

The Ultimate Gift — Jim Stovall

The Extraordinary Character of Winston Churchill; The Faith of the American Soldier; The Faith of George W. Bush — Stephen Mansfield

Your Best Life Now; Become a Better You; Every Day a Friday — Joel Osteen

The Other Side of Suffering — John Ramsey with Maria Chapian

It's All About Him — Denise Jackson with Ellen Vaughn

Everything I Know About Business I Learned at McDonald's — Paul Facella with Adina Genn

Call Me Ted — Ted Turner with Bill Burke

Halftime — Bob Buford

Three Feet from Gold — Sharon L. Lechner and Greg S. Reid

Celebrating Success — Gerard Smith

Audition: A Memoir — Barbara Walters

The Everything Law of Attraction Book — Meera Lester

Sundays at Tiffany's — James Patterson and Gabrielle Charbonnet

The Prayer Chest — Joel Fotinos

Harmonic Wealth — James Arthur Ray

Trust Your Gut — Lynn A. Robinson

The Millionaire Next Door — Thomas J. Stanley and William D. Danko

The Servant — James C. Hunter

Tough Times Never Last, But Tough People Do!; *Life's Not Fair but God Is Good*; *Tough-Minded Faith for Tender-Hearted People*; *Success Is Never Ending: Failure Is Never Final*; *The Be (Happy) Attitudes* — Robert H. Schuller

Win Forever — Pete Carroll

Leadership Beyond Reason — Dr. John Townsend

Going Rogue: An American Life — Sarah Palin

The Go-Getter — Peter B. Kyne

Heaven Is for Real — Todd Burpo with Lynn Vincent

Today We Are Rich — Tim Sanders

Power Thoughts — Joyce Meyer

Start Something That Matters — Blake Mycoskie

The Power of Purpose — Richard J. Leider

Your Road Map for Success — John C. Maxwell

Retraining the Brain — Dr. Frank Lawlis

The Pursuit of Holiness—Jerry Bridges

Good to Great — Jim Collins

The Law of Attraction — Esther & Jerry Hicks

Blink: The Power of Thinking Without Thinking — Malcolm Gladwell

The One Decision — Judith Wright

The Bondage Breaker — Neil T. Anderson

Waiting: Finding Hope When God Seems Silent —
Ben Patterson

Metaphysics 101: Manifesting Your Dreams —
Calvin Lehew

Diary of a Player — Brad Paisley and David Wild

Among the many lessons I've learned is that a lifetime is very, very short. But it is short for everyone. In the quest for success, for meaning, for growth and wisdom, time is the great equalizer. Someone else may have more talent, more energy, or more money, but no one has more time. It is the one  commodity you and I and Bill Gates all have in exactly the same amount.

The secret to success is using that time wisely. Within the pages of this book, you will see how my journey taught me the lessons that enabled me to succeed in the world of business and, I hope, in life. It has been a very good life. It hasn't been without its terrible tragedies—my older son, my namesake, was killed while still a young man—but God has been faithful and has been with me during the good times and the bad. I am grateful for the many, many blessings I have received, and this book is my attempt at sharing those blessings.

———⟨∞⟩———

Randall Baskin was founder, president, and CEO of Continental Life Insurance Company and American Continental Insurance Company. He is a motivational speaker, a firm believer in education, and a philanthropist who has given millions of dollars for the betterment of others.

———⟨∞⟩———

Rob Simbeck's work has appeared in *The Washington Post, Guideposts, Rolling Stone, Field & Stream, Free Inquiry, Country Weekly,* and many other publications. He is the author of *Daughter of the Air* and has been author, editor, or ghostwriter of fourteen other books.